HOLY
GATHERINGS

A Leader's Guide
for Engaging the Congregation
in Corporate Worship

HOLY
GATHERINGS

**Michael Sharp
and Argile Smith**

Outskirts Press, Inc.
Denver, Colorado

Holy Gatherings
A Leader's Guide for Engaging the Congregation in Corporate Worship
All Rights Reserved.
Copyright © Michael Sharp and Argile Smith
V3.0

Outskirts Press, Inc.
http://www.outskirtspress.com

ISBN: 978-1-4327-4074-0

Library of Congress Control Number: 2009927691

Outskirts Press and the "OP" logo are trademarks belonging to Outskirts Press, Inc.

PRINTED IN THE UNITED STATES OF AMERICA

CONTENTS

ACKNOWLEDGMENTS

A number of people helped us to write this book. Without their help, we would have never gotten this project off the ground.

The New Orleans Baptist Theological Seminary faculty and administration supported us while we worked on the book. They offered insights and suggestions that made it better.

The students enrolled in our courses deserve credit too. The raw material for the book came from endless hours of lectures, discussions, and debates over the theological foundation of worship leadership and its application in the churches. The hours spent with them and because of them enriched the final product beyond measure.

Our interactions with students in Cuba made a remarkable impact on us as we developed the manuscript. Teaching the truths of Scripture about worship in their setting proved to be one of our most rewarding adventures. Seeing worship through their eyes taught us more than we could ever teach them.

We are also indebted to others who encouraged us along the way. Pastors and other worship leaders along with people in the pews offered us useful perspectives that flavored the manuscript.

Sandra Galey performed a minor miracle when she took the rough – and we do mean *rough* – copy of the manuscript and cleaned it up into its present form. We owe the readability of the book to her. The obstacles to it belong to us.

PRELUDE

The manuscript you hold in your hands is the product of our extended involvement in the theory and practice of worship leadership. For some time now, we have been engaged in research into worship theory, and we have reached some significant conclusions that have shaped our thinking about this critical topic. For an even longer period of time, we have been involved in leading worship, one of us as a pastor-preacher and one of us as a minister-musician. Across the last thirty years, we have learned some valuable lessons about how God's people encounter Him in worship. As professors, we have enjoyed the privilege of comparing theory and practice and merging the insights we have gained into classroom lectures designed to guide students in their preparation as worship leaders in the church. This manuscript has been written in keeping with the rare privilege we have been given.

It's not the last word we will ever offer on the subject. As we completed the writing process, we isolated other topics still needed to be addressed. But for now, we are pleased to offer you what we have written so far. We hope that this resource will benefit you if you are a seminary student who is preparing for ministry in a church in which you will lead God's people to worship Him. Also, we anticipate that it will help you if you are a minister of a local church who is burdened about leading your people in meaningful, authentic worship. Likewise, we think that it will help you if you are concerned about discipling your people to grasp the theological foundation and expression of healthy worship as a congregation.

We thank the Lord for giving us His strength and direction as we have worked on this writing project. And we trust Him to use what we have written for His glory.

Michael Sharp, Ph.D.
Argile Smith, Ph.D.

CHAPTER 1

Describing Worship: What Is It?

How would you define the word *worship*? That's an important question because a definition helps us to comprehend a concept. Once we comprehend an important concept like worship by defining it, we can move on to helping people put the concept to work in their relationship with God.

But defining worship can be easier said than done. Books and articles on the subject of worship have proliferated in the last few years, and the definitions published in the literature have been extremely vast and diverse. Some of the definitions portray worship as a *lifestyle* while others treat it as an *event*. Still others reflect in their definitions that an understanding of worship involves a little bit of both.

Where do we begin in order to get the most helpful insight into the best definition of worship? Of course, we affirm that the Bible gives us the first and final words about worship. The following Bible texts help us to understand more about worship. Although none of the passages gives us the last word on what it means to worship God, each of them gives us a clearer picture of what worship involves. Taken together, they provide remarkable clarity regarding God's intention for us as we worship Him.

Worship Involves Surrender
Genesis 22:1-18

As we read the story about God commanding Abraham to kill Isaac as an act of worship, our first reflex is to recoil. Isn't worship supposed to be an uplifting experience? Doesn't God want us to enjoy being in His presence? How can worship involve something as painful as sacrificing your child? What good can come from that kind of worship experience? The answers to these kinds of questions come in whispers from the story itself, so pay close attention.

God's Strange Command

The story begins with God giving Abraham a strange command. God commanded Abraham to take Isaac up on a mountain and to sacrifice the young boy there. God's command doesn't make any sense because He gave Isaac to Abraham and Sarah, both of whom definitely qualified as senior adults when the baby came along. When God called Abraham to leave his homeland and go to a new place, Abraham was 75 years old (Gen. 12). Although he and Sarah had no children, God promised him that he would be the father of a great nation.

When Abraham was 100 years old and Sarah was only ten years younger, Isaac was born to them! After twenty five years, God fulfilled His promise and gave Abraham a son.

Now God ordered Abraham to sacrifice Isaac. It doesn't make sense to us. God's command to Abraham must have been confusing to him too.

This story does not represent the first time or the last time that God has directed His people to do things in worship that didn't make sense. Have you ever been led by the Lord to do something that broke your heart when you thought about doing it?

According to the first part of the story, God gave this strange command to test Abraham. God placed him in a situation in which he would have to choose either to surrender to God or to disobey

Him. Like He tested Abraham, He puts us in similar situations that challenge us to respond to Him with complete surrender.

How did Abraham respond to God's strange and painful command? Did he run in the opposite direction? Did he rebel? Did he try to give God another idea about what he could do to prove his loyalty? Did he question God? No. Early the next morning he arose and made the necessary preparation for the awful journey from his home to Mount Moriah.

Abraham had learned through a number of difficult experiences in his past that the best response to God's command was obedience, even when the command didn't make sense. Earlier in his life, he tried to respond to God's leadership by doing what he himself thought was best. For instance, God told Abraham to leave his people behind and go to a new place (Gen. 12:1). What did Abraham do? He carried his nephew, Lot, with him, which proved to be a terrible mistake! Lot gave him plenty of trouble more than a few times.

Also, Abraham decided to keep on going south after God had commanded him to stop in the new land. In fact, Abraham went on to Egypt. There he created a real mess for himself when he got involved in a lying scheme. Consequently, Pharaoh himself threw him and Sarah out of the country by ordering soldiers to escort them to the border (Gen. 12:20).

A Response of Surrender

By the time Isaac came along, Abraham had learned the hard way that obeying God was best, even when he could not understand the command given to him. For that reason, he didn't argue with God. Somehow he understood that the Lord knew what He was doing. His choice was simply to trust God and surrender to His way.

So he and Isaac began to make the heartbreaking journey to Mount Moriah. We don't know everything that they said to one another along the way, but we know that God didn't speak to Abraham to reassure him as he and Isaac traveled toward the mountain. The two of them walked along together those three long days while God remained absolutely silent.

Then they saw the mountain. That's when Abraham told the servants that he and Isaac would continue their journey alone. He added that they would worship God once they got to the mountain (Gen. 12:5).

How do you associate sacrificing what you consider to be most precious with worshiping God? Such an act of sacrifice can only be described as excruciating. Letting go of what we treasure most can be a gut-wrenching experience. As this story shows us so far, worship can be gruesomely painful instead of something fun and uplifting. Sometimes it becomes the hardest thing we could ever do, a journey into the presence of God that we can come to dread.

On the journey, Abraham showed his faith in God as well as his willingness to surrender to Him (Gen. 22:7-8). Isaac asked his father about the sacrificial lamb for the offering. He had watched Abraham at worship enough to know that a lamb had to be sacrificed. He knew that they had everything except the lamb. Where was the lamb?

Notice Abraham's only answer: God would provide. Abraham had no clue that God would allow his son to live. Yet, he had learned from walking with God that He could be trusted. Somehow, he would see God's hand at work in the confusing command that he would obey even though he couldn't make sense of it. The agonizingly painful journey called worship involved surrender that gave way to simple trust.

Then came the most difficult part of the worship experience. Abraham took Isaac, his son whom he loved with all of his heart, tied him up, and prepared to slaughter him. Isaac had carried up the wood for the altar, and Abraham had carried up the fire and the knife. Now those three implements would be used together to bring to an end the life of an old man's precious son. Moses had dared to call it worship.

The more we hold on to something, the more we think that it actually belongs to us. God has placed in our hands many precious people and resources. But none of them really belongs to us. From the perspective of the Bible, we do not actually possess anything. All we have has been given to us as a stewardship. The longer we hold on to the treasures God has placed in our lives, however, the more we think we own them.

When God tells us that He wants to take them from us, we do not want to do it at first. Letting go hurts us. But worshiping God involves surrendering to Him the precious treasures He has placed in our hands. Abraham had learned to obey the Lord without question. We can ask God to help us obey Him, too.

Painful as it must have been, Abraham obeyed God and attempted to offer his son on the altar. But as Abraham found out, God never really wanted Isaac's corpse; He wanted Abraham's life.

When Paul wrote to the Corinthian Christians, he had to deal with the church's bad attitude toward him and the offering he asked them to collect for the struggling Christians in Jerusalem. As he reprimanded them, he added, "What I want is not your possessions, but you" (2 Cor. 12:14). Paul expressed God's heart about the treasures that He takes from us. Ultimately, God doesn't want what we have when He calls on us to surrender; He wants us.

The God who provides calls us to worship Him by prompting us to give up what we treasure most. When we surrender our most precious treasures to Him, we trust Him to know and do what is best. And we find joy in the blessings of being obedient.

Abraham left Mount Moriah that day with his son, telling the story about how God had provided. The angel who stayed Abraham's hand also told him about the blessing to come because of his obedience. Abraham would be the father of a great nation, just like God promised. Abraham's family would be blessed and be a blessing to others. Because of Jesus Christ, we still enjoy that same two-fold blessing.

According to 2 Chronicles 3:1, God led Solomon to build the temple on Mount Moriah. Generations later, not far away from that very temple, God offered His own Son as a sacrifice. God provided the perfect sacrifice for us by allowing His Son to die on the cross for us. Again God provided, this time in a perfect way. He gave Christ so all people everywhere could receive His gift of salvation.

As a believer, you know that Christ is the greatest blessing we will ever receive. We are more than blessed, thanks to the sacrifice of God's beloved Son for us. The surrender involved in our worship pales in comparison to the sacrifice God made for our salvation.

That's why the main character in this story is not Abraham or Isaac, but God. When Abraham walked simply by faith, he may have wondered what God was doing. But by the end of the story, he rejoiced in the Lord who provided.

And so can we. As we worship, our surrender to Him leads to the blessing of knowing Him as the Lord Provider.

- How often has your worship experience involved the painful but necessary response of surrender?
- In the midst of obedience, how have you seen the Lord provide for you through Christ?

Worship Involves Relationship
1 Samuel 15-16

A religion can be described as an organized system of beliefs that its adherents embrace. Many such systems exist in the world today, and each one defines its own beliefs regarding what it values. The specific ideas which are valued in a particular religion are the elements which characterize the nature of that religion.

Although it may well be classified as a "religion" because it possesses an organized belief system, Christianity transcends the concept of religion because it is based upon a personal relationship between God and an individual. The potential for a relationship with God was hard-wired into human creation from the very beginning.

Throughout its pages, Scripture reveals that God desires a relationship with His human creation. The relationship is defined by a covenant God makes with His people in which He promises to bless them in many ways. Bountiful harvests, protection and safety, peace in the land, victory over adversaries, and family prosperity are some of the blessings mentioned in Leviticus 26. The covenant required obedience as God's people were to follow His decrees and obey His commands. The covenant is summed up as the Lord said: "I will walk among you and be your God, and you will be my people" (Lev. 26:12). The "I will...you will" syntax of that statement has relationship written all over it! But an essential ingredient in the divine-human relationship has obedience to the Lord as the centerpiece.

Worship and Disobedience

Chosen by God to be Israel's first king, Saul was given a mission. As he went up to battle the Amalekites, he was instructed by the Lord to take no prisoners. He was to destroy completely every one of the enemies as well as everything they possessed. They were not to bring back any spoils. Period. But fast-forward one day later to the post-battle scene as Samuel the prophet visited the victorious Saul. With the background noise of bleating sheep and mooing cows, Saul gladly greeted Samuel and assured him that he had carried out the Lord's instructions (1 Sam. 15:13). Already aware of Saul's disobedience, Samuel began to question Saul as to why he had not obeyed the Lord. Saul argued that he had indeed obeyed God. In the interest of worship, however, he had decided to bring the best of the livestock back with him to sacrifice before the Lord. Samuel must have found it unbelievable that Saul could be so arrogant. His reply to Saul provides us with a wise lesson on worship as well as on what happens when God's instructions are not followed:

> Does the LORD delight in burnt offerings and sacrifices as much as in obeying the voice of the Lord? To obey is better than sacrifice, and to heed is better than the fat of rams. For rebellion is like the sin of divination, and arrogance like the evil of idolatry. Because you have rejected the word of the LORD, he has rejected you as king (1 Sam. 15:22-23).

What a terrible cost for not following instructions! God seemed to be saying, "Saul, you're fired! How can you possibly lead the nation to honor God when you yourself are so careless in honoring what He asks of you?"

The story shows us that God values a relationship over a religion. Respecting the relationship with Him means honoring what pleases Him. Caring about the covenant means knowing and following what He desires. Engaging in empty religious activity is a poor substitute for the life-giving covenant relationship that is available to us. In the realm of true worship, sincere submission trumps empty sacrifice, and obedience means more than offering. No wonder the story moved quickly to a country shepherd boy who had a heart like God's. He would be anointed as Israel's next king.

God Looks at the Heart

At first glance, Samuel would probably have anointed Eliab, David's oldest brother, as Israel's next king. Tall and handsome, Eliab just looked like he would make a good king. Eventually Samuel would work his way through the roll call of Jesse's sons until he came to David, whom he anointed as Saul's replacement. Why David? Only God could look at the heart and know for certain the real depth of this young boy. At the moment, only God could see that David would place the highest priority on his relationship with his God for the rest of his life.

Intimacy with the Almighty

God has always pursued a relationship with people, and He has gone to great lengths to make Himself accessible to anyone who would desire a relationship with Him through His Son, Jesus Christ.

How can we have an intimate relationship with God who is not our equal, but our superior? We prefer to forego such a question about intimacy with God and go straight to a set of actions or religious deference, thus reducing worship to a religion and not a relationship. The answer to this probing question can only be found in how a holy God sees us.

Apart from Christ, we can know only the judgment of God. Consequently, we can never hope to enter His holy presence. Even so, many people have spent their lives doing religious things with the hope of somehow convincing God of their goodness. But the Bible teaches us that "without faith it is impossible to please God" (Heb. 11:6). The faith to which the passage refers is belief in Jesus Christ as our only hope of having a right relationship with God. Like Paul said, "Therefore, there is now no condemnation for those who are in Christ Jesus" (Rom. 8:1).

The ability to worship God begins when a person enters into a relationship with Christ. This relationship forms the only basis upon which a person can come to know God and rightly worship Him. This is the essence of the Good News! No longer do we need to offer sacrifices in a religious ritual. Christ has done everything necessary for us. Through faith, we come to God in worship, and He sees us as blameless.

Worship: Ritual or Relationship?

Worship goes awry when it demonstrates, in any form, that our behavior earns us some merit before holy God. Honorable actions like worship attendance, financial giving, singing in the choir, teaching a Sunday School class, worthy as they are, can lull would-be worshipers into a false security – thinking they have worshiped when, in fact, they have only completed their worship to-do lists. They may have performed their religious duties with no thought whatsoever about a personal relationship with God. Worship ritual without relationship is empty and lifeless. Perhaps this fact can explain why a church might be powerless and ineffective in the kingdom, despite holding endless "worship services." By contrast, worship actions fueled by a vibrant relationship with Jesus Christ can have transforming effects upon the life of the believer. This kind of worship will never leave us the same. Paul said it best: "And we, who with unveiled faces all reflect the Lord's glory, are being transformed into his likeness with ever-increasing glory, which comes from the Lord, who is the Spirit" (2 Cor. 3:18).

- What does your worship say about your personal relationship with God?
- How do you show that Christ alone has made you right with God?

Worship Involves Encounter
Isaiah 6:1-8

At first glance, Isaiah's testimony about his life-changing worship experience seemed simple to grasp. One day at the temple he encountered the Lord (Isa. 6:1). What happened to Isaiah as a result of the encounter, however, can only be described as a radical spiritual transformation. For that reason, Isaiah's testimony of his encounter with God that day provides a framework for designing worship experiences in which people meet God in a way that transforms them.

Seeing the Lord

Isaiah described what he saw when he found himself in God's presence. The Lord appeared above Isaiah. God's elevated position suggested His majesty and dominion. His robe filling the temple portrayed His regal presence. Isaiah beheld God as all-powerful, bigger than life, and majestic.

The Lord had angelic servants to minister to Him. They submitted themselves to Him by covering their faces in the presence of the Most High God. Covering their feet also indicated submission to Him as well. They flew at His bidding and according to His direction. Then Isaiah heard the angelic servants as they shouted praises to God, declaring His holiness and His glory in all of the earth.

What Isaiah saw and heard was the angelic response of praise to God. It's the same kind of praise that Jesus taught us to give to the Lord when we pray. (Matt. 6:9). Jesus' instruction shows us the necessity of praising God in worship. If we begin our personal or corporate time of worship with praise, we give ourselves an opportunity to recognize God's holiness, strength, royalty, and honor. That's why praise can become an exhilarating experience! The more we praise Him, the more we enjoy praising Him. Praise opens our spiritual eyes to the glorious Father we worship.

In Isaiah's testimony about worship, praise gave way to reverence. The shouts of the angels created a holy noise that caused the doorposts and the thresholds to shake. A humbling moment indeed, as God's presence shook the building to the very foundation! At the same moment, smoke filled the temple. A visible sign of the presence of the invisible God flooded the worship center as His glory could be sensed everywhere. Such a display would lead any believer to respond with hushed reverence, a holy fear associated with being in the presence of Almighty God.

Seeing Ourselves

Before Isaiah saw the Lord that eventful day, he might have seen himself spiritually as a person absolutely satisfied with himself. He might have become somewhat arrogant, like the Pharisee in Jesus' parable who stood in the middle of the temple generations later and expressed his spiritual arrogance in the form of a prayer to himself. (Luke. 18:9-14).

Something happened to Isaiah's perspective of himself, however, when he saw himself in the presence of the Lord. As Isaiah continued to tell the story of his encounter with God and worship, he described two important experiences. Both of them had a remarkable impact on him as he worshiped God that day. We can count on them to have the same result in our lives too.

First, Isaiah experienced deep grief over his sin. In the presence of God, his sinfulness had finally become as clear to him as it had always been to the Lord. When he recognized his sin, he lamented with a broken heart.

Isaiah acknowledged that he saw himself as a doomed person in the presence of God. So do we when we worship God in a transforming way. In the presence of God, we have no room for spiritual arrogance or pride. Being in His presence forces us to behold the honest portrayal of ourselves as sinners.

God didn't leave Isaiah mourning in his spiritual bankruptcy. Read Isaiah's testimony and notice that an angel of the Lord took a lump of coal from the altar and placed it on his lips. The coals heated the fire of atonement in the temple. Placing a coal on Isaiah's lips purged Isaiah's sin. For the first time in his life, Isaiah knew the joy of being forgiven. His sin had been taken away, never to be remembered again, thanks to God's wonderful mercy and grace.

How do you see yourself spiritually? In the presence of God, we cannot be arrogant and prideful. In His presence, we recognize that we are spiritually bankrupt. If we have received Christ, however, we also know that we have been pardoned (Rom. 5:1). What Isaiah knew well, Christians today know even better. Christ paid the price for our sin so we could be set free to serve the Lord with everything that's in us.

Hearing God's Voice

Isaiah's eyes had been opened to God and then to himself. Now he was ready to hear God's call. Before he encountered the Lord in worship, he probably would not have heard the Lord speaking at all. Now, with his eyes open, he could be sensitive to God's leadership in his life.

Isaiah listened as God made His divine appeal for His people to go in His name. Down through the generations, God has continued to issue that same call to believers everywhere. Jesus expressed the Father's call to go when He told His disciples to pray for the Lord to send forth workers into the harvest (Luke 10:2). He also expressed God's passion for reaching people when He gave His disciples the commission to go into the world and bear witness (Acts 1:8).

Isaiah would have never heard God's call if he hadn't experienced the Lord through life-changing worship. If he had remained in his spiritual arrogance, he would have been deaf to God's voice. The worship experience opened his eyes and made him attentive to God's direction for his life.

Worship prepares us to hear God's marching orders for us. That's why an encounter with God through personal as well as corporate worship plays such a vital role in our walk with Christ.

- What's your testimony about worship being a transforming encounter with God?
- How have you expressed in worship your awareness of your sin and your gratitude for God's salvation?

Worship Involves Reverence
Luke 5:5-10; Acts 9:3-9; Revelation 1:12-18

Who *is* this God whom we seek to worship? The way we answer this question has a strong correlation with our worship practice. Throughout the history of the church, believers have lived in the inevitable tension produced by two paradoxical truths: God's full nature is beyond human comprehension while, at the same time, God desires a personal relationship with each individual whom He has created. On one hand, Holy God is transcendent, beyond the grasp of finite minds. He is *knowable* to the extent to which He reveals himself to humankind, but He can only be partially comprehended from an earthly perspective. Yet, He has revealed Himself to us through His acts of creation (Rom. 1:20); through His Word (2 Tim. 3:16); through His Incarnation (John 1:14); and through His Holy Spirit (John 16:13).

A quick review of some of the people to whom God revealed Himself in the Bible turns up some striking parallels, all of which indicate that getting a glimpse of God's transcendent character consistently produces a sense of reverence. Notice throughout the

Bible that when individuals find themselves in the presence of the Almighty certain things begin to happen.

As we mentioned earlier, Isaiah caught a glimpse of the awesome majesty and glory of Almighty God in the temple and *responded in awe and holy fear* as he cried out, "Woe is me!" (Isa. 6:1-5). Moses also encountered the Lord – calling to Him from a burning bush, and the Bible indicates that Moses not only removed his sandals because of the holiness of the place but also *hid his face from God* (Ex. 31:5). After that incredible fishing expedition with Jesus (with such a large catch that they had to call for reinforcements), Simon Peter *fell at Jesus' knees and said "Go away from me, Lord; I am a sinful man!"* (Luke 5:10). We remember how Saul, who persecuted the early church, encountered Jesus on the Damacus road and was blinded by the light of the Lord's presence. *His response was to fall to the ground* (Acts 9:3-9). And the Apostle John, banished to the Isle of Patmos, received a vision of the Lord and *"fell at his feet as though dead"* (Rev. 1:12-18).

Mysterium tremendum

All of the individuals mentioned in the previous passages experienced an overwhelming sense of the holiness of God – a recognition of the truth that God is unlike any other reality and is set apart. Seeing God as incomprehensible, the worshiper encounters the *mysterium tremendum* – a sense of awe, reverence, and holy fear in His presence.

For each individual, catching even a glimpse of the transcendence of Almighty God was generally accompanied by a sense of spiritual frailty and shortcomings. It precipitated the need to respond to Him with great humility and submission.

Nothing has changed. God still is our Creator and sovereign Lord of the universe. He is set apart and above all created things. Worshiping Him in spirit and in truth (John 4:24) requires us to recognize the fact that he is both immanent *(God with us)* and transcendent *(God beyond us)*. The challenge lies in attempting to maintain both of these perspectives in balance. The danger of emphasizing one aspect to the exclusion of the other is either to fear God without the knowledge of His sacrificial love for us or to denigrate Him to our level – one who is the ultimate friend, without the recognition of His supremacy over all things (including us).

Cathedrals and storefronts

At various times throughout church history, the transcendence/immanence pendulum has swung to either extreme with serious consequences. Consider the history of worship space as an example. Until the fourth century, the church did not have organized structures in which to meet. Beginning with Constantine's rule, however, elaborate cathedrals were built – giving visual representation to the transcendence of God. Fast-forward to twenty-first century America and find newly-built worship centers which resemble warehouses, complete with warm, inviting atmospheres – intentionally aiming to communicate that God is accessible. Even the present day debate over *contemporary* versus *traditional* styles may be said to stem from the same transcendent/immanent dichotomy.

God is *both* transcendent and immanent. Understanding and embracing both truths fosters an authentic understanding of the worship of the Sovereign God who desires an intimate love relationship with those whom He has created. A line from the lyric of the song *Meekness and Majesty* by Graham Kendrick beautifully illustrates the point:

> O what a mystery, meekness and majesty;
> Bow down and worship, for this is your God.[1]

Healthy Results

A healthy church doing the work of worship will embrace the intimacy of a love-relationship with the Lord and testify to the life-changing power that is available through Him. Worshipers will be guilty of neither *worship-lite* or *worship therapy* with its "what-feels-good" barometer of what is acceptable worship. Advertising worship services on the church signage as "casual worship" will be a thing of the past. No longer will worshipers pseudo-actively register their attendance at a worship service while remaining disengaged from the reality that God loves them and desires an intimate relationship with them.

Striving for Balance

Take a look at your current worship practice in light of the two ideas: transcendence and immanence. Observe everything you can, including the following factors that contribute to worship: the architecture and physical surroundings of the worship space, the formal or informal design of the worship service, and even the contents of the worship service. Did these seem to emphasize the fear and awe of God or the concern and love of God? Notice the styles of presentation via music selection and instrumentation, the preaching style, and the usage of art and symbol. Take note of the involvement of clergy versus lay leaders, and other factors such as the use of choirs versus smaller praise teams, and the wearing of robes versus individual dress. Many of these considerations come to mind when we think about balancing God's immanence with His transcendence in worship. Regardless of the number of features we list, the key is working through them in order to accommodate both a sense of reverence for God who is The Almighty as well as a relationship with our Heavenly Father.

- How have you tried to accommodate the *mysterium tremendum* of worship?
- What are some of the ways you have expressed both reverence and relationship in worship?

Worship Involves Perspective
Matthew 17:1-7

As Jesus worked with His disciples, He guided them to encounters that would help them grow as followers. In the transfiguration experience, He guided three of the disciples to a mountain so their perspective of Him could be changed as they worshiped Him.

The story does not begin on the mountain itself but in the region of Caesarea Philippi. After Jesus led the disciples there, He asked them an important question: "Who do people say that I am?" (Matt.16:13).

They replied to his question with a variety of titles, all of which were complimentary. But none of them came very close to His correct identity.

Then Jesus asked His disciples, "Who do you say that I am?" (Matt.16:15). His question to them was most emphatic. It was by far the most important question that He ever asked them up to that point.

The angels in heaven must have held their breath as they waited for one of the disciples to answer His question. If the disciples did not understand it correctly, the Kingdom mission that centered in Christ would be in serious jeopardy. Everything depended on them answering the question correctly.

Simon Peter spoke up for the others, declaring, "You are the Christ, the Son of the living God" (Matt. 16:16). The angels in heaven must have rejoiced with His answer. Jesus certainly rejoiced and affirmed Simon for his declaration. It reflected the fact that God had opened Peter's eyes to the truth about Jesus' identity.

Later on in the same conversation, though, Peter said something else to Jesus, but this time what he said could not be considered complimentary. For the first time, Jesus told His disciples about going to Jerusalem and being killed and rising from the grave (Matt. 16:21). What did Simon Peter say in response? He rebuked Jesus! Can you imagine someone doing such a thing to the Son of God, the Messiah?

To the Mountain

At that point Jesus saw that Peter still needed to have his perspective corrected. So did the other disciples as well. They had their minds on their own concerns, and their concerns shaped their perspective about Jesus, who He was and why He was with them.

That's why Jesus took Peter, James, and John to a high mountain about six days later. With Peter's confession and rebuke fresh on their minds, Jesus took them up the high mountain to get them away from the distractions. There they could focus on Him.

A mountain appears to be a good place to change a person's perspective. Moses met God on a mountain while he was tending to sheep on the day he saw a burning bush. God spoke to him in that encounter and called him to lead God's people out of captivity in Egypt (Ex. 3:1-12).

Elijah met God on a mountain too. He had been courageous on Mount Carmel to confront the priests of idolatry. Then fear gripped him as he heard Jezebel's threat, and he ran for his life. To help the weary prophet regain his focus, God took Elijah to a mountain. There Elijah heard God speak in a brand new way, in the gentle blowing of the breeze (I Kings 19:11-13).

On the Mountain

There on the mountain with the disciples, both Moses and Elijah appeared with Jesus and talked with Him. Moses personified the Law, and Elijah personified the Prophets of the Old Testament. Their presence on the mountain with Jesus signaled to the disciples that the entire Old Testament pointed to Jesus as the Messiah.

Jesus stood between Moses and Elijah, but He looked different. His face glistened like the sun, and His clothes cast a brilliant white glow. The bright white light of Jesus' countenance reflected the glory of God's presence and affirmation. Of the three individuals standing together, God's glory rested only on Jesus. The visible presence of the invisible God on His Son sent a message the disciples should have grasped.

But they missed it altogether. Simon Peter spoke, and as he spoke he demonstrated he had missed the meaning of what he beheld as Jesus, Moses, and Elijah stood before him.

He said, "It is good for us to be here" (Matt. 17:4). Who would disagree with him? What would be better than being there at that moment? What would be more meaningful than to behold Jesus standing as the fulfillment of all that the Law and the Prophets promised about God's Messiah?

But what Peter said next showed that he had missed the point of the display altogether. Trying to capture the moment, he wanted to build three tabernacles. In Peter's day, Jewish people would build tents as a part of a yearly festival to remember the way God delivered His people from Egyptian bondage. To help them remember the wilderness experience of their ancestors, they would build tents and stay in them throughout the festival. Peter wanted to apply the ritual to his experience on the mountain. He was searching for a way that would allow him to enjoy the fellowship of Jesus, Moses, and Elijah for as long as he could. Perhaps he had in mind staying right there on the mountain and never coming down from it.

Peter's response gives us insight into what can happen in our worship. We can find ourselves worshiping the experience of worship itself. The mountain-top experience of worship can become something we don't want to leave. Like Peter, we can place our attention on the experience or the moment of worship and overlook the Savior who deserves our wholehearted devotion.

Simon Peter did not get to finish his suggestion about the tabernacles. While he was talking, the bright cloud appeared and hovered over them all. The cloud reflected God's glory for all of them to see. A voice spoke from the cloud. The voice had spoken at Jesus' baptism. It was God's voice, affirming Jesus as His beloved Son. Now, on the mountain, God's voice added a command, "Listen to Him" (Matt. 17:5).

Three figures were seen together at the transfiguration, but God told the disciples to listen only to His Son. Simon Peter had talked and talked about things related to the experience of being there. But the Father wanted him – and the others – to hush their chatter and to listen to His Son.

Listening continues to be a challenge in our communication with one another. Instead of listening, we simply take turns talking. It's a bad habit in human communication. It's an even worse habit for us to develop in our communion with the Lord.

Listening to Him means that we must be quiet. It means that we need to spend time in His Word, meditating and reflecting on it. It also means that we need to learn to be still and wait for Him to speak to us before we ramble on with our own words.

When the disciples heard the voice out of the cloud, they fell to the ground in terror. The voice had silenced their talking. Finally they were quiet.

Jesus approached them in their fear and touched them. He told them not to be afraid because He was there with them. When they looked up, they no longer saw Elijah or Moses. They only saw Jesus. As Matthew put it, they saw "Jesus Himself alone" (Matt. 17:8).

Down the Mountain

A week or so earlier Simon Peter had declared on behalf of the other disciples that Jesus was the Christ, the Son of the living God. Then almost immediately he rebuked Jesus. On the mountain he wanted to spend time with Jesus, but he wanted to include Moses and Elijah. Now, finally, He wanted to worship Jesus alone.

James and John needed to see Jesus in the same way because the time would come for them to return to the other disciples down the mountain. There they would encounter a number of challenges. Who would guide them to know how to handle them? *Jesus Himself alone.*

Who would show them the love of God by extending His hand of healing and His arms of love? *Jesus Himself alone.*

Who would set His face toward Jerusalem at the right time to make His triumphal entry into the Holy City, signifying that the Prince of Peace had come? *Jesus Himself alone.*

Who would allow Himself to be the object of a mock trial by religious leaders who wanted to kill him? *Jesus Himself alone.*

Who would allow Himself to be beaten and mistreated? *Jesus Himself alone.*

Who would make His way up the winding road toward Golgotha, carrying a cross on which He would be nailed, so He could be the substitute for our sin? *Jesus Himself alone.*

Who would die on that cruel cross so we could have eternal life? *Jesus Himself alone.*

Who would rise from the grave on that first Easter morning so that you and I could have victory over death? *Jesus Himself alone.*

Who would ascend to the heavens after giving us His command to bear witness of Him to all of the world? *Jesus Himself alone.*

What matters most in worship is not the mountain-top experience, but seeing Jesus alone. So instead of chasing after another experience of worship that transfixes us on a higher mountain of jubilation, we do well to worship God in a way that reshapes our perspective on His Son, our Savior, Jesus Christ.

- Who has influenced you to center your focus in worship on Jesus alone?
- How have you learned to listen to Jesus as you worship Him?

Worship Involves Regard
John 12:1-8

How do we measure how much something actually means to us? By what means do we discern the value of a relationship? Sometimes we gauge the worth of something by how much we are willing to pay for it, or by what we are willing to do in order to obtain it. In all honesty, the saying *"Put your money where your mouth is"* underlines the unvarnished reality that talk can be cheap and therefore not a realistic measure of what is truly valued. What we say doesn't always reflect what we really believe.

We can say we appreciate a certain type of music. But a more accurate assessment would note how much actual interaction we have had with the music. For example, how much money did we spend on recordings, or how often did we tune in to the radio station or attend concerts where that music was featured? It is one thing to say it and quite another to express it through observable behavior.

And yet, it's much the same with our regard for God. The question for each worshiper is, and should be, how highly do I regard God? The honest answer to that question speaks volumes about our worship of Him. One of Jesus' disciples illustrated this in a beautiful way.

Jesus Came to Her House

Jesus was no stranger to the home of Lazarus and his two sisters, Mary and Martha. On several occasions Jesus spent time with them, enjoying their warm hospitality and friendship. One of the few times mentioned in the New Testament in which Jesus wept referred to the death of his friend Lazarus. And one of the most astounding miracles Jesus ever performed was to raise Lazarus from the dead after he had been entombed for four days! Obviously this family meant a great deal to Jesus, as He did to them. During Jesus' last visit to their home, before the events leading up to his death, burial, and resurrection, Mary honored Jesus with an extravagant expression of worship. What Mary did signified the high regard she held for her Lord.

On this occasion, while Lazarus and Jesus were at the dinner table and Martha was in the kitchen, Mary came and knelt at Jesus' feet. She took an expensive, fragrant oil and anointed Jesus' feet with it. Afterward she wiped his feet with her hair. Her actions communicated the supreme regard she had for Jesus. But it was not without cost.

No Cheap Offering

Judas was quick to point out the value of that pound of ointment. He assessed the fragrant substance to be worth about a year's wages for a common worker of that day. No one would doubt that her gift represented a lot of money, poured out and used up in just a few moments. Some would use the word "wasteful" to describe it. Even Mary would not dispute that it was costly. But that was not the point. She was thinking with her heart about how she could truly express to her Lord how much He meant to her. And perhaps she had been really listening as Jesus spoke about going to Jerusalem. Everyone knew that journey would be dangerous, since the Jews were anxious to get rid of Jesus. Perhaps Mary sensed the urgency of this expression to minister to her Lord. We don't know. But we do know that this outpouring of love and regard for Jesus was costly – a year's wages.

How highly we regard God can often be observed in the quality of the things we offer Him. Our minutes, our money, and our mental energy are just a few of the resources we have to offer. Our regard for God is linked to the outward expressions of our lives on so many levels. Authentic worshipers can't imagine bringing left-overs to God, or bringing offerings with no cost involved. David, the man after God's own heart, wouldn't hear of offering to God something that cost him nothing. Araunah offered to supply the oxen, the supplies, and even the field for David to sacrifice to the Lord. David's reply was noteworthy: "No, I insist on paying you for it. I will not sacrifice to the LORD my God burnt offerings that cost me nothing" (2 Sam. 24:24).

What Will They Think?

Sometimes the expression of regarding God highly can be costly in terms of what others think! The account of Mary's fragrant offering also tells us that Judas was not happy about it. In fact, he began to rebuke Mary, insisting that her actions were wasteful and detrimental to the community of the poor! Imagine Mary's humiliation as Judas expressed his indignation. Sometimes the expression of our love for the Lord will result in repercussions from people who see it. As Mary experienced, a personal rebuke might follow quickly as someone comments on our so-called near-sighted actions. Even a well-meaning individual might remind us that at some time in the future we will surely regret having given away what we gave to the Lord. But worship that holds our Lord in the highest regard doesn't worry about that. It is worship that knows that here and now is temporary; heaven is eternal.

- How can a Christian show his or her high regard for God in public worship?
- What prompts Christians at worship to show their regard for God?

Worship Involves Confidence
Philippians 3:3

Paul's statement in Philippians 3:3 provides us with a principle that should help us put into practice the truths we have encountered in our study of other Bible passages about worship.

Paul wrote this verse to a congregation he loved with all of his heart. Some troublemakers apparently had disrupted the congregation with the notion that being a Christian meant following some religious rules and regulations. To set the record straight on the matter, Paul insisted that being a Christian involved transformative worship.

The word *worship* that Paul used in this verse can also be translated *serve*. The word signifies that worship and service are actually two sides of the same coin. Accordingly, we worship when we serve, and we serve when we worship. The word also suggests that worship is a lifestyle before it's an event on Sunday at church. As a lifestyle, serving and worshiping God become first priorities for us each day.

We Worship in the Spirit of God

When we gather together at church for worship, we seek an encounter with Him. When we serve Him as an act of worship, we seek His pleasure in our work. But we don't worship or serve Him all by ourselves. His Spirit helps us.

God created us to worship Him. And our greatest joy comes when we worship Him with our whole hearts. He knows that we need to worship Him, so He prompts us to meet with Him in private and public ways. Privately He pulls at our hearts, encouraging us to find the time and the place to be with Him. Then He opens our minds and hearts to His presence and His direction for us as we focus attention on His Word.

We Glory in Christ Jesus

If we are led by the Spirit of God in worship, we will always be drawn to Christ Jesus, the centerpiece of our worship. He is the vine who supplies everything we need in order to flourish spiritually. As Paul stated in Colossians 1:18-19, Jesus is the head of the church. The church's life and direction come from Christ, and all of the fullness of God dwells in Him as well. Consequently, He is the only way to experience the fullness of God's presence. When we worship, the Lord Christ becomes the center of our attention because He alone nourishes us and gives us direction. And He alone helps us to experience the fullness of God's presence.

That's why Paul identified Christ as the object of a believer's joy. God intends for us to rejoice – or glory – in Him alone in our worship.

Sometimes believers fall short of God's intention in worship. Too often we find ourselves rejoicing in other things as we worship, and most of them center in ourselves. For example, we tend to rejoice in our accomplishments. We glory in the fact that we have grown spiritually. Likewise, we can be tempted to rejoice in ourselves when we accomplish a monumental spiritual task. Such self-glorification can produce spiritual arrogance.

In our worship we may also be tempted to rejoice over what's happening in our church, but in a self-glorifying way. Rejoicing in what Jesus has done in a church is certainly appropriate. However, when we boast about our church's accomplishments like they depended on us alone, our rejoicing is misplaced. We may say that our church is huge, our church is wealthy, or our church is the best. But in our hearts we may not be boasting in what Jesus has done. Rather, we may be boasting about what we have done to make the church huge, wealthy, or the best.

Indeed, we can glory in many things other than Jesus Christ. But Paul teaches us that true worship brings glory to Him. A stanza from an old hymn expresses well the glory of Christ we are meant to experience when we worship:

> There is sunshine in my soul today
> More glorious and bright
> Than glows in any earthly sky
> For Jesus is my light
> Oh there's sunshine, blessed sunshine
> When the peaceful, happy moments roll
> When Jesus shows His smiling face,
> There is sunshine in my soul.[2]

That song speaks of the way we glory solely in Christ Jesus. Instead of calling attention to anything we have done, our joy is directed to Jesus. As we worship, we warm ourselves in the glow of His presence. That's the way we find true joy in personal as well as corporate acts of worship and service.

We Put No Confidence in the Flesh

Paul teaches us that we can be confident as we worship. God's Spirit will lead us to rejoice in Christ Jesus. However, we should not have the same confidence in what we bring to the table as we worship.

What did Paul have in mind when he talked about *the flesh*? Read the next few verses and you will get a hint as to the answer. Paul gave his biographical sketch in detail, which, by the way, was most impressive. If you had been an employer in search of someone with a trained mind and proven leadership skills, you would probably have hired Paul on the spot after studying his resume. He was born in the right area, a member of the right religious group, educated in the right schools, belonging to the right organization, and demonstrated the right kind of passion for his religious work.

Yet, he said that all of these credentials counted as nothing more than rubbish in contrast to his relationship with Jesus Christ. He did not express any confidence in any of his credentials, impressive as they might have been to the people of his day. That's what Paul had in mind when he wrote about having no confidence in the flesh.

But Paul's attitude begs a few questions. Was Paul's Jewish background helpful in his missionary work? Yes. Was Paul's theological training useful to him as he blended the Old Testament truths with his encounter with the living Christ? Absolutely. Did Paul's zeal for God, reshaped by Christ, have a positive impact on his Kingdom work? Without a doubt.

No, Paul did not discard what he had learned along the way from his encounter with Jesus on the road to Damascus. In fact, as a Christian missionary he put everything that happened to him to good use and for God's glory. He stopped putting confidence in himself, however, once he placed his complete trust in the Lord Jesus Christ.

Why did Paul put no confidence in his credentials? Because he knew that *the flesh* would fail. In the same way, if we put our confidence in what we bring to the worship service, we will eventually be disappointed. Think about it for a moment. We bring a number of items to worship: songbooks, screens, microphones, choirs, chairs, rooms, traditions, preferences, and habits of worship. If we place our confidence in these tools for worship, eventually we will be disappointed because worship tools by themselves do not move us into the presence of Christ.

Worshipers in underground churches around the world meet

God as they gather together. They do not have most of the tools we use often, and yet they have meaningful worship experiences every time they gather.

Our fulfillment in worship cannot depend on all the right tools being present. We use them if we have them, but not having them will not prevent us from life-changing worship. Our confidence rests in the assurance that the Spirit of God will prompt us to rejoice in Christ Jesus. Even though we may bring to the table a number of useful items that serve as tools to help us in our worship, we know for certain that we can worship without them. Our confidence in worship doesn't come from having them in the worship center.

- Where is your confidence placed when you worship?
- How has God's Spirit guided you recently in worship?

So, What is Worship?

The foregoing passages only scratch the surface of insights provided in the Bible regarding what's involved in worship. They represent the vast range of scriptural principles associated with worship as a lifestyle and as an event. Taken together, they show us that coming up with a comprehensive definition of worship can be next to impossible. How can we define worship in a way that includes everything that's involved in understanding it? Can we squeeze such important components like surrender, relationship, encounter, regard, perspective, reverence, and confidence into a line or two that will capture what worship actually means by definition?

Instead of crafting a definition, perhaps we would be better served by settling on a description of worship. If we choose to describe a reality instead of defining it, we would certainly be in good company. Jesus defined very few realities related to our walk with Him; He chose to describe them. For instance, Jesus never really defined the Kingdom of God; He described it. And He described it in a number of picturesque ways. He said the Kingdom of God was like a precious stone in the middle of a pasture, a mustard seed, a landowner who hired laborers throughout the day, or ten virgins waiting for a wedding to begin. Of course, a list of His descriptions would be quite long and extensive, but you get the point. Jesus preferred to describe the realities of our relationship with Him. Following His example, settling on a description of worship seems to be a good idea.

So, how can we describe worship? To answer that question, consider the common denominator in each of the Bible passages considered so far. What do all of them have in common? Each of them has something to say about an encounter with God. Or to put it in other words, all of them are about a person or people meeting God.

Starting there gives us a concrete description of worship. Stated simply, *worship is meeting God*. Some people may prefer to describe it another way: *worship is encountering God*. Either way, an important point about worship becomes clear. Whether we consider worship as a lifestyle or an event, it's all about meeting God in a way that has a life-changing effect on the people who encounter Him. That encounter involves important issues like surrender, relationship, encounter, regard, perspective, reverence, and confidence. Such a description of worship may be simple, but it's also elegant enough to set us thinking about worship in a productive way.

If we embrace the description of worship as meeting God, we choose a concrete word picture, or a metaphor, in the place of an abstraction. For most of us who are struggling with a place to begin the consideration of worship, a concrete picture is worth more than a thousand abstract words.

The description of worship as an encounter with God provides us a basic picture that can be shaped and colored by the Bible passages that relate to it. Using the Scripture texts we have highlighted so far, we can color worship as an encounter with God that calls on us to surrender to Him, to nurture a relationship with Him, to seek an encounter with Him, and to reflect our high regard for Him. It's a meeting with God that prompts us to focus our attention on His Son, our Savior, Jesus Christ, in reverence and confidence that He will help us as we seek to worship Him.

What Is Worship Leadership?

The description of worship as a meeting with God not only gives us something of a conceptual framework, it helps us get a better grasp of the role played by a worship leader. Ordinarily, a person who stands up in front of other people to speak or sing assumes the role of a performer. As a performer, how you speak or how you sing become the objects of attention for the people who are listening and watching you. In the end, you accept the fact that such attention is associated with evaluation. Consequently, you tend to perform in a way that will render a positive evaluation from the people who compose the audience.

At the core of the assumption, however, is a critical component that should not be present in worship leaders. Ultimately, worship leaders don't perform to be evaluated by the people they lead in worship. Even though worship leaders sing and speak in worship services, they are not performers in the fine arts sense of the word. They are more like prompters. Through our songs and symbols, our worship designs and architecture, our expressions and our intercessions, we prompt people to have a meaningful encounter with God.

So much more from the Bible can be said about worship and worship leadership. Many other helpful descriptions and prescriptions related to worship can be found in the Bible. Also, a rich assortment of Hebrew and Greek words that are translated as *worship* in the Bible opens our minds and hearts to the contours of the encounter with Him that we hunger and thirst for as we grow in our relationship with Him. But we are off to a good start with a basic picture that can be painted in rich detail with the vast insights from God's Word. And as worship leaders, we have a clear path for our work. We have been called to prompt people to meet God in a life-changing way. When we consider this calling in the context of corporate worship, how do we as leaders approach our leadership task? In the next couple of chapters we will explore some of the issues involved in planning for these "holy gatherings"—regular times of worship in which the church assembles together with the expectation of encountering our living God.

CHAPTER 2

Designing Worship:
How Do We Plan It?

The First Steps

Chris always seemed to have a clear impression of what he wanted in a worship service. Ever since he had become a Christian in college, he had enjoyed the worship experiences in the church where he was baptized. When God called him to ministry, his experiences in his church during those formative years as a growing believer had definitely shaped his ideas about how worship should be done. At seminary, he immersed himself in the study of worship. He read all of the books on worship theory he could get his hands on, and he embraced the theories that reinforced his convictions about a dream-come-true kind of worship experience.

In his first ministry setting, however, he learned a hard lesson about putting worship theories into practice. He discovered that turning his dreams about worship into realities in a local church could be downright difficult, and sometimes next to impossible. Chris soon realized not long after he began his ministry in his church that you cannot simply snap your fingers and make your worship dreams come true. Loads of work must go in to designing worship services that offer an opportunity for the people in the congregation to meet God.

A dream-come-true worship design that can be superimposed over any congregation in a one-size-fits-all fashion doesn't exist.

The congregations that gather for an encounter with God in worship bring with them an assortment of cultural diversities which makes them all unique. A better approach involves designing services with a particular congregation in mind. Such an approach may take a little time to perfect, but it will be worth the effort.

Developed in keeping with what the Bible teaches us about worship, the following approach offers a useful plan for developing a workable design for worship in your congregational setting. You and the other worship leaders in your church can start with this basic plan and then expand on it as you grow in your insights and skills for planning worship services for your church.

Isolate the Elements

The first step in the plan is to get a firm grasp on the elements at hand for a worship leader to use in the worship planning process. If you think about a worship service as a path along which people are led to an encounter with God, the elements of worship are the stepping stones. They are placed in an order that will allow the people to move from one point in worship to another. Thinking of the elements of worship in this way will strengthen your appreciation of their value in worship planning.

The following elements serve as the basic stepping stones for worship leaders as they guide God's people through the experience of worship: Scripture, praise, music, prayer, offering, sermon, and invitation. These elements have been described well in a number of leading resources on worship leadership.[3] Consequently, this list probably doesn't have many surprises for worship leaders. These stepping stones of worship have been used by God's people in worship for generations, and each of them has rock solid scriptural footing.

Think about the unique role to be played by each one of the elements. Consider how they add to the meaning of worship for the congregation and the worship leader. Also, factor in the reality that they take on different and probably deeper meanings over time as God's people worship together. So don't discount the value of each element. In the right setting at the right time, the least of the elements just might become the greatest in a person's life-changing encounter with the Lord in worship.

Scripture

For centuries, God's people have given serious attention to His Word in worship. From the days of Old Testament worship until the present, the Scripture occupied an important place in the service, and with good reason! Something happens when a worship leader reads a passage from the Bible. The sound of the text being read in worship has a unique way of arresting attention and focusing minds and hearts on God.

So read it often. We expect the preacher to read a pericope as the basis of the sermon. But do we expect the Bible to be read in any other place in the service? With a little imagination, we can think of an assortment of ways to incorporate Scripture readings into the service. In so doing, we can also raise the expectation among God's people to hear the reading of His Word when they gather to worship Him.

At what points in the service do you read Scripture? Think about reading a Bible passage to begin the worship service. A wide variety of passages lend themselves well to being read at the beginning of worship as a way of drawing the attention of the people away from themselves and others and on to God Almighty. Try reading passages like Psalm 24:3-4, Psalm 118:28, Isaiah 55:6-7, John 4:23-24, or Revelation 3:20. Better yet, ask someone in the congregation to be prepared to read one of these texts in worship.

Incorporate Scripture readings into the conclusion of the service. Some excellent Bible benedictions can be used by worship leaders interested in helping God's people step out of the worship center and into the mission field of their community. Passages like Philippians 4:23, 2 Corinthians 13:14, Ephesians 3:20-21, Jude 24-25, and Hebrews 13:20-21 are excellent choices for the worship leader or the entire congregation to read at the end of the worship service.

Don't forget to use the Bible at other places in the worship service too. Read an appropriate passage in connection with the offering, as a transition from one feature in the service to another, between songs, or in any other way that will do justice to God's Word in worship.

Scripture passages used in worship deserve to be read well. Reading God's Word in worship poorly doesn't do justice to the text, the worship service, the congregation, or the Lord who has given us the Scriptures. On the other hand, well-read Bible portions can have a remarkable impact on the people gathered for the worship service.

Preparation for Scripture reading requires only a little effort, and the benefits certainly make the effort worthwhile. Basically, it involves reading the text aloud in private before it is read in public. This kind of rehearsal helps you to be able to enrich the reading by giving a voice to the inflections embedded in the syntax and punctuation marks in the text. And it enables you to work on pronouncing the tough person and place names that may be found in the passage.

Praise

Praise has always been an element of worship for God's people.[4] Over the past few decades, however, the potency of praise has been rediscovered. Worship leaders and congregations have come to find a new appreciation for the awesome power of praise and the way it functions in the worship service.

When we praise God in worship, we express our awareness that He is the Lord. Praise enables us to adore Him, marveling at the splendor of His majesty and sovereignty over all creation as well as the intimacy of His mercy and grace to us through Jesus Christ. Both aspects of God's character – His splendor and His intimacy – lie at the heart of our praise to Him. Helping people to embrace these twin features of God's character as they praise Him lies at the heart of effective worship leadership.

Through the tremendous element of praise, we set out to come into the presence of God and see Him as He really is—sovereign Lord and loving Father. In turn, we see ourselves as we really are—frail human beings who don't deserve Him. Like Isaiah, who was deeply moved by seeing the Lord and the seraphim praising Him, we see ourselves as sinners who need to be forgiven (Isa. 6:5). And like Isaiah, we see ourselves as forgiven because God has removed our sin (Isa. 6:6-7). But unlike Isaiah, we know about the sacrifice of Christ on the cross for us. Because of Christ, we have a more refined perspective on what God has done for us in order to save us from our sins.

Praise moves us to express our joy because He has forgiven us by His grace. When we embrace afresh through praise the power of our gracious Lord calling us to worship Him and the mystery of His intimacy with us through Christ, His joy fills our minds and hearts. The joy inside us finds expression with the words and actions of praise.

Because of the tremendous power of praise, seasoned worship leaders have learned to handle this crucial element with care. Indeed, praise helps to avoid the spiritual arrogance that characterizes God's people when they lose sight of Him and His sovereignty and His grace. Ignoring praise to God can lead God's people to become spiritually arrogant. In time they find themselves patting themselves on their backs, spiritually speaking, as they themselves become the objects of their praise in the wake of forgetting God. That's why praise plays a critical role in helping God's people to stay focused on Him.

On the other hand, a congregation at worship can become distracted with the expressions of jubilation associated with praise. Consequently, they can find themselves searching for the jubilation for its own sake instead of worshiping the Lord as the object of their delight. Certainly jubilation makes worshipers feel wonderful, but jubilation without direction can have a damaging effect on worship. A worship experience that should center on Christ can be turned into an emotional soiree that's focused only on the experience itself. Worship leaders who have learned this fine distinction do everything they can to keep the Lord the centerpiece of the praises of His people. Only in that way will praise fulfill its intended function in worship.

Because this element has become such a topic of discussion among worship leaders, more attention will be given to it in Chapter 4. For now, though, we do well to see that praise belongs in worship and that it has a vital function in the life of a worshiping congregation.

Music

While the issue of what kind of music has caused an extended debate among Christians, very few believers would disagree that music ranks high on the list of worship elements. Travel to any part of the world and worship with God's people there, and you will hear music and be prompted to sing.

Of all the elements, music has the most obvious footing in Scripture. In the Old Testament, worshipers embraced music as a chief tool to express their public as well as private worship of God, and they made music with the instruments available to them at the time and with their voices as they sang to the Lord. The Book of Psalms has been referred to as the first hymnal for God's people. It covers the spectrum of life circumstances and worship experiences with songs of high praise along with poetic expressions of worship in the face of deep lament. In the New Testament, the emphasis on singing in worship continued to be underscored. For example, Paul encouraged the Colossian church to give attention to singing with a grateful heart to the Lord (Col. 3:16).

Like praise, music in worship has always captivated the attention of worship leaders. In the past few decades, the literature on the subject has flourished, and the discussions have become more intense and provocative. The association of music with other expressions of worship has put an even finer point on this vital worship element. For these reasons, more attention will be given to music in worship later in Chapter 4 as well.

Prayer

Prayer has also been one of the most prominent elements in worship perhaps because of its versatility. Think about the number of ways in which prayer has been incorporated into worship services you have attended. You have also seen that prayer in worship takes on a variety of forms.

The *gathering* prayer has also been referred to as the *invocation*. It's the prayer voiced by the worship leader at the beginning of the worship service. Usually a very brief but pointed prayer, it focuses the congregation's attention on the reality of the presence of God. In fact, the prayer at its best affirms God's presence in the service. The prayer also involves asking Him to help the congregation to recognize His presence and to respond to His leadership in the worship experience.

The prayer of *confession* also plays an important part in meaningful worship. Once God's people find themselves in the presence of God and become aware of who He is, we have a clear picture of who we are in His presence. Like Isaiah, we see ourselves as sinners who are undone and incomplete. And also like Isaiah, we rejoice in the grace of God who forgives us. Of course, what Isaiah knew well about his sin and God's forgiveness, we who have received Christ's gift of salvation know even better. We know that Christ's sacrifice on the cross paid our sin debt, giving us new life in Him. Accordingly, we confess our unworthiness because of our sin, and we confess our faith in Christ whose sacrifice made us worthy to be called God's children when He saved us.

Therefore, a prayer of confession voiced by a worship leader on behalf of the congregation means confessing two great realities: our sin before God and our faith in Christ. When the congregation hears the worship leader offer such a prayer of confession, they will be able to keep the foundation of their relationship with God in sharp focus. If they are reminded of His great grace in Christ who paid the debt of our sin, they are less likely to grow arrogant and apathetic in the way they approach Him in worship and the way they serve Him with their lives.

Intercession is another common form of prayer in worship. This form of prayer helps us to focus our attention to others in our congregation and around the world who need what God can supply. Intercessory prayer links us up with the people we pray for, and it gets us outside ourselves as we worship. After all, in the Lord's Prayer, Jesus taught us to pray in terms of *we* and *us*, not *me* and *I*. Granted, praying for our own needs has a distinct place in personal and public worship. But transformative worship takes place when we get outside ourselves and pray for others.

The ways God's people intercede for others in prayer during worship are usually shaped by the culture of the congregation involved in intercession. In some churches, the altar call provides an opportunity for people to intercede for others. In other churches, congregations dissolve into groups of three or four people who pray together – sometimes holding hands with one another and sometimes on their knees. Still other churches incorporate silence as the back drop of intercession. With a prayer list in hand, the people at worship engage in quiet intercession, speaking to God heart to heart about the individuals whose needs have been brought to their attention.

The *pastoral* prayer can also have a significant place in worship, especially when a congregation faces a crisis. Using this kind of prayer, the pastor talks to God on behalf of his congregation, taking the concerns of his people to the throne of grace. The people hear every word of their pastor's prayer, although he's not talking *to* them but *about* them to God. Therein lies the secret of the lasting impact of a pastoral prayer. The people hear their pastor lift them up in prayer, sometimes individually and at other times collectively, with a heart of loyal love for them.

For previous generations, the pastoral prayer played such an important role in worship that some pastors would write word for word what they intended to use as they stood to pray in the worship service. Across the years, many of their written prayers have been published. Read them and you get the distinct feel of a pastor's agony over what to say to God in the presence of His people. Over time, the discipline of preparing for the pastoral prayer gave way to a preference for more extemporaneous and even impromptu utterances in prayer. Whether impromptu or scripted, the pastoral prayer deserves a prominent place in the ministry of the pastor as a worship leader.

Prayer associated with giving as an act of worship takes a unique form too. The *offertory* prayer gives the congregation the privilege of thanking God for His blessings, the most important of which is the gift of His Son. It can also reflect the willingness of God's people to surrender their resources to Him in the awareness that ultimately He owns everything.

A *benediction* or closing prayer provides an opportunity to ask God's blessings on the worshiping community as they depart to serve God throughout the coming week. This prayer may also include a plan for God's help as worshipers respond in service to what He has shown them during the worship experience. Some Scripture passages can be used effectively as a benediction such as the Aaronic blessing found in Numbers 6:24-26: "The Lord bless you and keep you; the Lord make His face shine upon you and be gracious to you; the Lord turn His face toward you and give you peace."

Offering

Some people don't quite understand the role of the offering in the service. They consider passing the plate in worship to be little more than a necessary inconvenience. For that reason, they're frustrated with the way the service has to be interrupted in order to collect money for the church.

Actually, the offering as an element in worship has a firm foundation in the Bible. More than a few Old Testament passages refer to God's people bringing Him their offering as they worshiped Him. In fact, bringing the offering, and the tithe in particular, was a way of honoring God in worship.[5] In the New Testament, the best example of the offering comes by way of the church planted at Pentecost. In Acts 4:32-35, Luke gave the account of the believers being together in heart as well as in location and laying their offerings at the feet of the apostles. As an act of worship, laying their gifts at the apostles' feet represented the surrender of their money to the Lord for His use. In keeping with that worship action, the church used the money to take care of the needs of the people in the congregation.

Far from a nuisance, the offering needs to have an important place in worship. The offering is a time for God's people to express their gratitude for His indescribable gift of salvation through His Son, Jesus Christ. And it's a time for them to demonstrate their thankfulness for God's other blessings that have been theirs to enjoy because of His goodness and grace.

But the offering has another meaning for God's people as they worship. It's an opportunity for them to express with their offering the truth that God really owns everything they possess. That God has given us what we possess is a basic principle of stewardship from James 1:17 that growing believers gladly embrace. Even if we have a deed to the property or a title to the car, we still recognize that, in the final analysis, we don't own anything. On the contrary, God has made us stewards of what He has given us. Our commitment to be good stewards of His resources can be renewed every time we participate in the offering during the worship service.

The offering can be more meaningful for the congregation if worship leaders take the time to think about ways of incorporating the theological realities about stewardship into the service. For instance, suppose someone leads the congregation in a prayer of gratitude to God for His blessings just before or after the offering is taken. Or imagine what would happen if the worship leader were to ask the people one Sunday to make their offerings as a tribute of their thankfulness to God for His great gift of salvation.

By the same token, suppose a worship leader led the people in the service to see their offerings as a symbol of the fact that God owned everything they had. What would happen if people were to see their offering in that kind of worshipful way? Instead of an interruption to worship, the offering would begin to be viewed as a critical juncture in the service.

Sermon

Pastors and congregations alike affirm the value of preaching as a critical element in effective worship. That's why the sermon involves a significant amount of time in most worship services. It's time well spent if the congregation and the sermon intersect at the point of an encounter with God through Christ.

In order for the sermon to become a more vital element in worship, however, four basic convictions must be embraced by the preacher. First, the sermon has to be drawn from a Bible text. For this and many other reasons, expository preaching continues to be the best approach to a pastor's pulpit ministry. An expository sermon finds its foundation – in content as well as in form – in a Bible passage that's been studied in light of sound principles of interpretation. Seasoned pastors everywhere have learned the value of the consecutive treatment of passages of Scripture to develop expository sermons. When they preach through an entire Bible book or an extended section within it, they know that people will hear God's Word in a way that can make a spiritual difference in their lives.

Second, the preacher has to see himself as a worship leader. Since the sermon is delivered in the context of worship, the preacher needs to understand that what he does in the pulpit is closely associated with what the other worship leaders are trying to do in the service. All of them as worship leaders share the common goal of nurturing an environment in which people in the pews can encounter God. That powerful reality forces a preacher to see the exposition as more than an opportunity to share correct information that's been arranged correctly into a sermon. It's an opportunity for God to speak to His people through His Word with life-changing possibilities.

Third, the preacher relies on the Holy Spirit to enable him to preach effectively. The Spirit opens the preacher's eyes to the truth of a text as he studies it for the sermon. And He enables the preacher to deliver the sermon in His power. At the same time, He works in the people sitting in the pews, affirming the authority of the truth proclaimed in the sermon in their lives. For that reason, a preacher who intends to be an effective worship leader through his sermon learns to depend on the Holy Spirit to give him what he can't give himself as he stands to preach God's Word.

Fourth, the preacher points to Christ in every sermon. In his heart, he bears the burden of delivering God's message of reconciliation through Jesus Christ. Implicitly or explicitly, every text in the Bible points to the same grand message. What's that message? Through Christ alone we can experience reconciliation; the walls between God, others, and even ourselves can come tumbling down. When the walls come down because people have turned to Christ, worship takes on a whole new meaning in the life of the church.

Invitation

You can't talk about preaching Christ in worship without bringing up the invitation. Granted, in many congregations, the invitation isn't included as a formal element of worship even though preaching may be considered to have a pivotal role in the service and the preacher shares the message of reconciliation through Christ in every sermon. In other churches, people have an opportunity after the pastor preaches the sermon to express publicly and immediately their responses to the Lord as He has moved them through the service. Although expressed in different ways, the need to allow individuals to respond to the Lord makes the invitation an important element in worship.

The invitation makes perfect sense when you think about the Good News. The proclamation about the gift of salvation through Christ demands an opportunity for people to receive it. For example, when Peter preached the sermon at Pentecost, people asked him what they had to do in order to be saved. After he told them about how they could receive Christ's gift of salvation, he appealed to them for a response. Three thousand of them responded to his appeal and received Christ (Acts 2:37-41).

The very nature of worship itself also makes a public invitation a good idea. Worship has already been described as meeting God, encountering Him in a life-changing way. When worship leaders design and lead services with that kind of encounter in mind, the people in the service must be given the opportunity to express what has happened to them, what the Lord has directed them to do, and their willingness to respond to His leadership in their lives.

The character of God gives us another excellent reason for including a public invitation in the worship service. Jesus painted one of the most profound and moving portrayals of God by using as His paintbrush the now popular story that we have named the Parable of the Prodigal Son (Luke 15:11-32). In the story, the father ran to meet the wayward son who had decided to come home after a long, hard learning experience in the far country. Arms open wide, the loving father embraced the boy, hugged him, restored him, and even called for a celebration in his honor. It's a fitting image of the loving God who invites us with arms open wide to come to Him. And it's a fitting way to think about what a public invitation can be for the people who need to come to the Lord.

As worship leaders lead their congregations in the invitation, however, they do well to take into consideration an important warning. The invitation lends itself to deep introspection, which can sometimes be associated with emotional extremes. Worship leaders can be tempted in that vulnerable moment to manipulate people. By using inappropriate persuasive tactics, they can coax people into making bogus public decisions based entirely on the manipulation of minds and not the conviction of the Holy Spirit.

In the face of such a tempting opportunity, wise worship leaders learn to trust the work of the Holy Spirit to bring a person under conviction and to prompt him or her to make a public response. Sometimes they learn that hard lesson by dealing with the fallout that always follows inappropriate appeals during the invitation. Over time, they observe that decisions made under the manipulative spell of a worship leader don't go very deep or last very long. By contrast, decisions made as a result of the conviction of the Holy Spirit usually render the evidence of a life changed, thanks to an encounter with God in worship.

Ordinances

Worship can supply Christians with some enriching images and symbols that crystallize our bedrock convictions about our relationship with God in Jesus Christ. Baptism and the Lord's Supper have remained for generations two of the most meaningful symbols of our faith. For Baptists, the Lord's Supper and baptism are not only rich symbols, they are ordinances to be taken seriously by the congregation. Because these ordinances convey such rich meanings, we do well to incorporate them into worship in ways that can reflect their value in congregational life.

Worship leaders face a notable challenge when they try to incorporate either of these two ordinances into a service. The challenge has to do with familiarity. At first, a new Christian experiences a sense of wonder about being baptized in obedience to the command of our Lord. Likewise, the first time a new believer participates in the Lord's Supper, the bread and the cup and the surrounding sights and sounds of worship invite a response both of joy and humility. Reflecting on the meaning of Christ's body and blood can bring tears to the eyes of a new-born child of God.

But in due time, these ordinances can become ritualized by a congregation. When baptism or the Lord's Supper becomes more like an empty ritual, either ordinance can lose its wonder for the worshiping community. Observing someone's baptism may have stirred the heart of a believer at first, but now it's all but overlooked as a special time in the worship service. In the same way, the Lord's Supper can become nothing more than an agenda item in the service. Taking the bread and the cup can lose its luster for the believer who lives on the verge of going through the motions of worship as a substitute for worshiping God sincerely.

The tendency toward ritualizing the ordinances in a believer's life can be aggravated by the habit of a distracted worship leader who includes the ordinances in the service as little more than afterthoughts or unwanted but necessary appendages. If the erosion of meaning regarding the ordinances continues unabated, the damage can have far reaching effects. Another generation of worship leaders who don't appreciate the meaning of these ordinances at all may be misled into deciding to clip the ordinances from the service altogether. For that reason, worship leaders today need to give due consideration to the ordinances as elements in worship.

The Lord continues to challenge us to take the Lord's Supper seriously as we worship Him (1 Cor. 11:17-34). Also Jesus commanded us to make baptism a high priority (Matt. 28:19-20). What can a worship leader do in order to retain the value of the ordinances for the congregation? Two suggestions come to mind.

The first suggestion is to devote an entire service periodically to one or both of the ordinances. Such a suggestion does not mean that all of the other elements have to be ignored. Rather, the other elements move the people at worship to a new appreciation for the rich spiritual realities bound up in observing the baptism of a new believer and/or taking the bread and the cup in remembering the Lord's death, burial, and resurrection. Of course, devoting an entire service to the ordinances will stretch the worship leaders to prepare exceptionally well, but the effort will be worthwhile. It promises to render a deeper, more lasting commitment to Christ within the worshiping community.

The second suggestion is directed to the pastor and his pulpit ministry. In the worship service in which one or both of the ordinances will be observed, a pastor may choose to prepare a sermon on a theme related to them. The Bible contains a wide range of themes that resonate with baptism and the Lord's Supper. Basic themes from the Bible about forgiveness, discipleship, relationships, surrender, unity, and eschatology fit well with the ordinances. With a little planning, a pastor can take advantage of the preaching and teaching opportunities every time the baptistery or the Lord's Supper table becomes a focal point in worship.

Other suggestions for worship leaders probably will come to mind easily because the rich meanings of the ordinances can be expressed in a number of ways. With just a little thought and planning, baptism and the Lord's Supper can be excellent elements for worship in which an encounter with the Lord can take place.

- Which worship elements seem to be most prominent in your church? Why?
- Why should we begin the process of worship planning with a clear understanding of the elements we intend to use?

Work with a Design Template

A good grasp of the elements to be used in a service lays a solid foundation for the other steps to be taken in worship planning. With the elements in mind, a worship leader can move to the next critical step of placing them in the service in a sequence that enables the congregation to move through the worship experience in which an encounter with the Lord can be accommodated.

Placing the elements into a sequence doesn't have to be a hit-or-miss task that worship leaders try to figure out on their own. Instead, it can be done according to some reliable patterns in the Bible. These patterns can provide the phases of movement necessary for meaningful worship to take place.

For instance, consider two texts of Scripture that relate to worship, one of them descriptive and the other prescriptive. They bear a striking similarity that's important for worship leaders to observe. If you compare Isaiah 6:1-8 with Matthew 6:9-13, you will notice some similarities between them. Isaiah 6:1-8 reflects some well-defined phases through which the soon-to-be prophet Isaiah moves in his life-changing encounter with the Lord. A similar kind of move can be seen in the Model Prayer in Matthew 6: 9-13. Take the time to study this and other Bible texts that have to do with prayer and worship, and you will notice the same movement occurring quite frequently. These similarities in movement give us helpful clues about a pattern for worship design.

The order of movement for worship and prayer found in Bible texts like these two passages serves well to provide excellent guidance for planning the meeting of the congregation with the Lord in a worship service. From the Scripture a basic template emerges that can be used as a reliable pattern for designing the worship service.

Based on Bible passages related to worship, the following template can be used to guide worship leaders as they arrange the elements of a service in a way that nurtures an encounter with the Lord. The template includes a sequence of seven phases to be considered in worship: *assembling, praising, confessing, focusing, preaching, inviting,* and *going.* Designing a worship service well means carefully factoring in each of the phases in a sequence that allows the congregation to move through the worship experience in a meaningful way.

Phase One – Assembling

The idea for assembling as the initial phase of worship comes from a number of Scripture passages. One of the most prominent is the observation made by Luke in Acts 2:1, that the disciples gathered together in one place. And in Acts 4:32, Luke pointed out that the post-Pentecost congregation was united spiritually and relationally. The picture painted by these descriptions has God's people together with their hearts and minds directed solely on Him.

When a congregation gathers together for the service, assembling them into a worshiping community becomes the first priority. The attention of the people has to be turned to the Lord. Granted, directing a person's heart to God is the work of the Holy Spirit, and a worship leader can't do His work in His place. Only God's Spirit can jostle us into awareness that we have come into the presence of the Lord. Under the Spirit's guidance worship leaders can capitalize on the opportunity at the beginning of the service to direct the attention of the people away from themselves and each other and to the Lord Himself.

In the twentieth century, worship leaders planned a powerful, captivating beginning into the design of worship services to gather the people's minds and hearts. They incorporated elements like music, Scripture, and prayer to fix the congregation's concentration on the reality of the Lord's presence in the worship service. Choirs, anthems, congregational singing, responsive readings, and invocations helped

God's people get off to a powerful start in worship.

As congregations have transitioned into the twenty-first century, the need for a strong beginning in worship has not diminished although the way it's expressed may be different. In many churches, it has become more pronounced as the cultural landscape of the congregation changes. Whereas twentieth-century people tended to favor an aesthetic approach to worship that assumed a certain amount of reflection, many twenty-first century believers tend to prefer kinesthetic worship that engages them from the soles of their feet to the tips of their fingers. Assembling them in terms of their minds, hearts, and bodies to come into the presence of the Lord demands that worship leaders be more intentional in the way they plan this first phase of worship. The same elements – prayer, Scripture, music – can be used, although the expression of these elements will be as different as the congregations that gather for worship.

Phase Two – Praising

After the people in the congregation have been led to turn their attention to the Lord, they should be guided to praise Him. They need to recognize that coming into the presence of the Lord means praising Him for his majesty and intimacy in His relationship with His people.

Although other elements of worship can be used to enable them to voice their praise and adoration to God, worship leaders seem to choose music almost always, and with good reason. Singing enables God's people to lift up praise to God by lifting up their voices together. Music gives them a way to express what they want to say *about* Him as well as what they want to say *to* Him in this important phase of worship. Both aspects of praising God are incorporated into a worship service easily by the use of well-chosen songs.

Of course, the choice of songs to be used to praise God will be determined in large measure by the culture of the congregation. Some congregations lean in the direction of aesthetic worship in which time for reflection is factored into the service. In aesthetic congregations, praising God means singing stately hymns of praise accompanied by musical instruments like a piano or organ. The hymns are sung one at a time, and sometimes the people are led to stand and then to sit as they sing. And sometimes they are led to stop singing and listen to someone pray. Leading God's people in this way enables them to reflect on what they are doing as they praise God.

Other congregations prefer to praise God in an interactive way. Instead of being aesthetic, they lean in the direction of kinesthetic praise. They favor the opportunity to stand before the Lord and to sing directly to Him, and they prefer to stretch their hands upward and close their eyes as they sing. For them, singing praise is done in one seamless phase that's not interspersed with stopping and going again or standing up or sitting down and then back up again. They want to sing loud, clap their hands, and shout as they praise Him. Instead of stately hymns, they prefer to sing vibrant worship songs that encapsulate their perspective on their relationship with God at that moment. They depend on the worship leader to choose songs that help them to find expression for the joy in their hearts because they are in the presence of God.

Most congregations have both kinds of people in them, and their different opinions about the best ways to express praise have been the sources of not a few problems for worship leaders. Designing worship that accommodates both groups can be difficult, if not impossible. But what makes the challenge more reasonable is the fact that the purpose of worship in general and praise in particular is not to please God's people. Rather it's to help them to meet God in a way that can change their lives. That theological reality shapes the decisions of seasoned worship leaders regarding the way they guide their congregations to praise Him.

Phase Three – Confessing

In the process of praising God, His people regain their perspective on who He really is in their lives. They see Him afresh as sovereign

Lord and loving Father. Seeing Him in that way has a profound effect on their perceptions of themselves. They see themselves as they really are before God, sinners who can do nothing in and of themselves to win God's favor. But at the same time they also see themselves as individuals whom God has forgiven through Jesus Christ. Because He has forgiven them, they now enjoy a relationship so intimate that they can call Him *Father* and see themselves as *His children*. Seeing themselves in these two ways deepens their worship experience, making it an opportunity to remember and rejoice over the gift of eternal life that Christ has given them.

Of course, not all the people in a worship service will see themselves as sinners who have been forgiven. If they have not received God's gift of salvation, they will have nothing more than the bitter awareness of their sin because they have not yet experienced His forgiveness. Until they repent and place their faith in Christ, they cannot relish the savory wonder of His forgiveness and the sweet taste of His grace. For that reason, we insist that some of the people who gather for worship may not be Christians. But at the same time we must also insist that being with God's people in worship can open their eyes to the relationship with God they need to have for themselves.

For God's people, however, the twin confessions of sin and salvation become the first critical turning point in worship. With it, God's people can continue to grow in humility and gratitude. Without it, however, they can become spiritually arrogant and anemic.

A variety of elements can be used to accommodate confession in worship. For instance, music can be selected that will express the heart of the people in light of the reality of God's gift of salvation through Jesus Christ. The selections could be congregational songs, choral or ensemble contributions, or solos. Also, a prayer of confession voiced by one person on behalf of God's people would be most appropriate. In addition, selected Scripture passages about what Christ has done for us to forgive us of our sin could be read either by one person or by the congregation as a whole. The worship culture of the congregation would determine which approaches would be most beneficial.

Phase Four – Focusing

Up to this point in the worship service, God's people have been led in worship to do all the talking. Through the phases of assembling, praising, and confessing, they have spoken and sung to and about the Lord. In the focusing phase of the service, they are led to listen to the Lord speaking to them. This phase of the worship experience involves the people focusing their attention on what the Lord will be saying to them through the sermon. By giving attention to this phase of the service, worship leaders prepare the congregation for the preaching of God's Word.

How can a worship leader guide the congregation through this phase of the service? One way is to include a song of testimony that's associated with the topic, the text, or the objective of the sermon. The song could be sung by a soloist, an ensemble, or the entire congregation. The important factor for the worship leader is that the song prepares the people for the sermon.

Another way of focusing the people's attention so they can prepare to listen to the preaching of God's Word is to include the reading of a Scripture passage that complements the sermon. Like the song, the selected text can be read by one person or by the entire congregation antiphonally, responsively, or in unison. Again, the purpose of this Bible reading is to heighten the congregation's awareness of the sermon text, topic, or objective.

Along with music and Scripture reading, prayer can be used to focus the minds and hearts of the people on the preaching of God's Word. A pastor praying for his people, asking God to help them as they listen to his sermon, can make a significant difference in a worship service. Other people can be enlisted to pray as well.

The visual elements of video clips or graphics on a projection screen or dramatic sketches can also help to focus people's attention on listening to God's Word. If the resources are available they can be used effectively to tie in to the theme.

All of these and other ways will be useful in helping the congregation to focus on the sermon. But their usefulness depends largely on the preacher sharing the important information about the sermon text and/or topic with the other worship leaders well in advance. For that reason, a pastor does well to develop a preaching plan that includes the text and topic for each sermon that he intends to preach over the span of a series of weeks or months, or even for an entire year.

The value of a preaching plan for worship leadership can never be overestimated. Along with many other benefits, it provides the other worship leaders with a long-range perspective. Accordingly, they will have the time necessary to gather helpful resources and incorporate creative worship expressions that can enhance the quality of this phase of the service.

Phase Five – Preaching

Now the time has come for the people worshiping to be still and listen to God as He speaks to them through the proclamation of His Word. Of course, being still doesn't imply complete silence or passivity. It implies an important transition in worship. Before the sermon, participation in worship was reflected in a number of expressions that involved the worshipers' voices and bodies. But as they listen to the sermon, participation on the part of the people takes the shape of an eager mind, an open heart, and a submissive will. While they may be free to be no less expressive, the nature of the sermon prompts them to listen so they can internalize what God's trying to say to them.

If you preach in worship, you bear a heavy responsibility as a worship leader. The worship service has been guided to direct God's people to what He will say to them through the proclamation of His Word. Now it's your turn. You have been given the challenge of proclaiming it, telling them what God says. It's an audacious task, one that can overwhelm you when you think about the reality that eternity is at stake for the people who listen to your sermon. God has brought them to the service and guided them to prepare their minds and hearts to hear from Him through your message. What they hear can make an eternal difference if they take it seriously.

That's why you must deliver the message well.

Because of what's at stake, you can't afford to squander the opportunity. For that reason, rethink the temptation to begin your sermon with a joke that has nothing to do with what you intend to say in the sermon. The other worship leaders have led God's people through the phases of worship leading up to the sermon. In so doing, they have placed in your hands a congregation ready to listen. Misguided preachers allow what's been handed to them to slip through their fingers when they begin their sermon by saying something to get a laugh for its own sake.

Wise preachers will take what's been handed to them and handle it with care. They will move carefully from what's been said or sung to what they need to say in order to transition God's people to the sermon text and the message from it. Of course, humor may be incorporated, but only if it's appropriate to the sermon and the worship service. Other rhetorical techniques may also be used, just as long as they help the preacher to deliver the Word of God well in the context of the worship service.

Phase Six – Inviting

The invitation can be treated as a worship element in a number of ways. In some churches, worship leaders include a formal opportunity for people to register publicly their responses to God as they have encountered Him in worship. In other churches, worship leaders don't provide a public invitation, but they invite people to talk with counselors in designated areas not far from the worship center. Still other worship leaders invite people to respond by noting decisions or questions on cards and dropping them in an offering plate or leaving them with an usher.

No matter how it's expressed, an invitation should be included to give people a moment to respond to God's direction in their lives as they have worshiped Him. Anticipate that the Holy Spirit will have convicted someone in the worship service of his or her need to receive God's gift of salvation through repentance and faith in

Christ. Also, a new believer in the service will be looking for a way to express childlike obedience to the Lord's command about baptism. Baptized believers whom God has led to connect to the congregation in membership will be there too. Members of the congregation who will be prompted by the Spirit to surrender themselves to the Lord in some specific ways will be looking for an opportunity to register their surrender. So will the person whom God has called to ministry. The invitation provides all of these people the focal point of decision.

As you guide God's people through this critical phase of worship, consider leading the invitation in two segments. The first segment will involve responses to the Lord that relate to the sermon. As you lead this segment, you will want to think through prayerfully the ways in which responses could be framed and expressed. The second segment will be more general. God's Spirit could lead a worshiper to do something that's totally unrelated to anything the preacher has said in the sermon or that the other worship leaders have included in the service. A broad invitation would accommodate the different responses God's people are led to make to His leadership in their lives.

Also, consider the reality that the invitation continues even after the conclusion of the worship service. Sometimes worship leaders get discouraged because they see few or no public responses during the invitation. Their discouragement can lead them to draw some inappropriate conclusions about themselves as worship leaders, their congregations, and God's work among them.

Actually, worship leaders can't ever know for certain all of the transactions that have taken place between God and His people in worship. Many of the most meaningful transactions may never be registered in the invitation time. At best, they will be reflected by people in more subtle ways: a stronger hand shake, a bigger hug, or misty eyes as they speak to you as they leave the worship center. Effective invitations don't always mean more people who make public decisions immediately. Only in eternity can the effectiveness of invitation times in worship truly be measured.

Phase Seven – Going

Maybe a better term for what happens at the conclusion of a worship service is *transitioning*. If worship makes a difference to God's people as they assemble, it will be reflected in what they think, say, and do as they go their way after the service. Worship as an event in the sanctuary has to transition into worship as a lifestyle.

What can worship leaders do to guide God's people to make that critical transition? That's an important question, given the temptation among worship leaders to finish the service with only a fizzle. A huge investment of creativity and synergy goes into planning and leading God's people to gather, praise, confess, and focus on what God's going to say to them through the sermon. An equally monumental amount of energy goes into preparing the exposition of God's Word and then delivering it passionately and persuasively. With the invitation, the climactic phase of worship, the service reaches a peak. Consequently, after the invitation the worship service might seem to just coast along in a kind of cool-down mode. By the time the worship leaders get to the end of the service, they can be tempted to treat what happens then as an afterthought instead of an important part of the worship experience.

In order to avoid such a temptation, consider the value of helping God's people transition from worship as an event to worship as a lifestyle. For example, the pastor could use the conclusion of the service to highlight one or two ways to put the sermon text into practice. Or the congregation could be led to sing a chorus that resonates with the theme of the worship service. Perhaps a worship leader might guide the people to quote – and maybe from memory – a Scripture text that will center their thoughts and actions as they serve the Lord as salt and light in the world. As they sing the chorus or quote the Bible passage together, they can be led to join hands across the worship center to reflect the value of each other in worship as an event as well as a lifestyle.

- What are some ways to apply this basic template for worship design in your setting?
- How can a congregation be led to understand the value of moving through each of the phases of worship identified in the template?

CHAPTER 3

Designing Worship: How Do We Plan It?

The Next Steps

You read about Chris in the previous chapter. He learned the hard way that designing worship services isn't easy. Fortunately, it's not as difficult when worship leaders like Chris follow some basic steps in the process. The first two steps have already been described. Now the next steps in the designing process can be considered.

Try to Settle on a Theme for the Service

The operative word is *try* because settling on a theme for the worship service may not always be possible in some cases. Either the worship leaders can't agree on the theme, or they don't see the value of the theme in the planning process. For example, many pastors don't favor the idea of developing a preaching plan, which is essential to purposeful worship planning. They prefer to keep their sermon topics and texts to themselves. Or maybe they have carved out a way of preparing their sermons that doesn't demand them to have a clearly stated sermon idea well in advance of Sunday. Without the information about the sermon, settling on a theme for the service can be difficult, if not next to impossible.

That's not the only reason why worship leaders have difficulty when they try to determine the theme of the service. Some of them consider every worship service to be about meeting God. For them, worship leadership comes down to that same goal every Sunday no matter what the pastor says in the sermon. They consider that goal to be challenging enough without the additional demand of planning worship services each Sunday around a specific theme. In their opinion, the theme of every service has already been determined by the very purpose of worship itself.

While such an argument against settling on a theme may have warrant, arguing in favor of it has merit as well. Determining the theme for the service allows the worship leaders to have a focal point for their creativity. Also, it adds a sense of variety to the services that prevents worship from getting in the dangerous rut of being done in the same way Sunday after Sunday. Furthermore, it promotes good stewardship of the resources for worship, both in terms of supplies and people. The selections in the church's music library can be put to better use, and so can the people who help in worship leadership every Sunday.

One more issue deserves attention at this point. Ideally, planning worship is a team effort. Later on in the chapter on transitioning worship, you will read about working with a worship leadership team made up of people who play a significant role in the effectiveness of a service. The reality of your ministry setting, however, may be quite different from the ideal. For whatever reason, you may be the sole worship leader, and the responsibility for planning worship rests on your shoulders alone. In one way, your situation makes this step much easier for you. But in another way, it presents you with a significant challenge. Creativity can be more difficult to nurture as a solo effort.

Several sources can be helpful to worship leaders as they try to determine the theme of a worship service. The first source has already been mentioned: the pastor's preaching plan. Pastors who plan their sermons help themselves and their congregations in a number of ways. Most important, they provide other worship leaders with critical information for planning the services in keeping with the themes of their sermon texts and/or topics. As stated previously, that kind of essential information enables other worship leaders to work more effectively as they plan worship. Musical worship leaders will require more long-range planning time as they secure resources and rehearse with music leaders weeks in advance for a particular service. Also, they have the fulfillment of knowing that they have played an active role in guiding God's people in worship, enabling them to focus their attention on the pastor's proclamation of God's Word.

A second source for settling on a theme for worship is the calendar. Or maybe *calendars* would be a better way to highlight this important source since it includes the secular, church, denominational, and Christian calendars.

The people in the congregation plan their lives around an assortment of secular calendar events. Worship leaders do well to be sensitive to those events so they can redeem them in the services. New Year's Day, Valentine's Day, Mother's Day, Father's Day, Independence Day, Veteran's Day, and Thanksgiving Day are among the most commonly observed special days on the American secular calendar. When God's people gather for worship on New Year's Day, for example, they bring with them ideas and images associated with it. Worship leaders who settle on a theme associated with the holiday can redeem the ideas and images for the sake of an encounter with God in the service.

The church calendar is important too, and it should be considered in the process of settling on the theme of a worship service. It shows the course the church has plotted for the year. Special emphases such as stewardship campaigns and missions services are usually reflected in calendar events. Worship leaders can benefit from the church calendar, and the congregation can benefit from the coordination of the worship services with the overall direction of the church. As an example of coordination between leadership of various ministries, one church produced a four-week devotional guide for their church members to coincide with the upcoming church's stewardship emphasis. It included an audio CD of a song for each week, and each song was used in the corporate worship gathering at the corresponding time. The efforts at coordination enriched the worship experience of those involved.

Along with the church calendar, a worship leader will be wise to consult the denominational calendar for input on a theme. The local church isn't an extension of the denomination. However, denominational linkage helps a local congregation to reach farther to make a Kingdom difference in the world. Accordingly, certain denominational events or efforts may provide promising themes for worship.

The Christian calendar also deserves some consideration. It's typically used by worship leaders in liturgical churches, but evangelical worship leaders have seen the value of some of the features of the Christian calendar and have incorporated them with positive results. A good example is the Advent season. The events of Passion Week have also been adapted well in evangelical worship services. Granted, evangelical congregations will always worship in the free-church tradition, but the liturgical church tradition can offer some promising ideas for worship themes.

Sometimes themes come along which leaders could not have anticipated. Two recent examples come to mind. On September 11, 2001, the terrorist attacks shook America, affecting every one of us. Worship leaders could not have anticipated such a horrible event as they planned worship for the following Sunday. But most churches took what happened as a theme for the service. Another example was the Sunday following the devastation caused by Hurricane Katrina in communities along the Gulf Coast and New Orleans. Although many congregations were unable to meet the following Sunday, the churches that could worship together gathered around the theme of dependence upon God in the midst of incredible destruction. The theme was not planned ahead of time, but it was there, overwhelmingly there. Sometimes worship leaders have a theme, and on certain occasions the theme has us!

- What's your opinion about settling on a theme for each service?
- Which of these sources of a worship theme seem to be used more in your church?

Develop the Theme in the Service

This step can be the most difficult for worship leaders who plan and lead worship services Sunday after Sunday in the same church. A long tenure as a worship leader of the same congregation presents a challenge to be creative. As seasoned worship leaders know, creativity can be in short supply in the context of the hard work associated with ministry in the local church ministry. Doing worship services the same way Sunday after Sunday is much easier.

The following suggestions may be helpful to nurture creativity in worship planning. First, think about the service from different perspectives. Seeing the same reality from a different angle can nurture creativity. It sparks imagination, which is essential to worship planning that's effective over a long period of time.

How do you see a worship service from a different perspective? Try looking at the worship service through a child's eyes. Children see their world in a fascinating way. Listening to them talk about what they see soon convinces you that God must be letting them use His eyes to behold what's going on around them. And He has also given them the ability to talk about what they have seen with striking, elegant simplicity. When a worship leader takes the time to see with a child's eyes what's going on in a service, the result can be a bundle of insights that can enrich the service.

You will also benefit from studying the service through the eyes of a teenager, a college student, a single adult, a single parent, or a senior adult. How can you accommodate yourself to such different perspectives? The key is to internalize the mindsets of the people in your congregation by putting yourself in their shoes as they worship.

One worship leader in particular gives us a good example of how it can be done. He takes the time each week to sit for a while in the empty worship center. Sitting in a different pew each week, he thinks about the people who would usually sit there and ponders what they must be seeing, thinking, and feeling from their vantage points as they participate in worship each Sunday. The moments in their pews give him some impressions about what he can do to lead them to an encounter with God in worship.

Second, work with what's really there in the congregation, and don't lament about what's missing. Worship leaders can make a mistake when they focus their attention on what's missing in their church. Suppose you dwell obsessively on the fact that your choir is not very well trained, the sound system is not adequate, or that a projector and screen aren't installed in the worship center. Before long, you may begin to make some inappropriate comparisons and draw some unhealthy conclusions about the potential for effective worship in your church.

The sad outcome of such a pessimistic perspective is that you will not see what's available to you for worship planning. No, you may not have a well-trained choir, but you may have a choir filled with people who enjoy singing together for God's glory. Similarly, you may not have a projection system, but you may have a congregation for whom technology doesn't matter as much as relationships. They have a high regard for you as their worship leader and for each other as brothers and sisters in Christ. As you grow to love your people and work with them, you will grow in discovering that those kinds of relationships in the congregation are far more valuable than even the best technical equipment in any worship center.

If you ask God to help you to see what's there, He will open your eyes to some ideas for worship that will fit the people you are trying to lead in worship. He will also help you to introduce the ideas in ways that will be productive for the congregation.

Inevitably, the subject of change comes up when worship leaders take seriously the critical step of developing the theme of the service. Changes in the way worship begins, the way the elements are presented, the leaders who are involved in the service, as well as many other changes always accompany the creative process of seeing what's there and putting it to work in the service.

Worship leaders who maneuver successfully in the troubled waters of congregational changes in worship lean on some basic realities. First, they don't necessarily expect God's people to resist change. Indeed, resisting change is a part of human nature, but growing believers are compelled by the character of Christ. If they are convinced that the change in worship is consistent with the Lord's direction for the congregation, they will usually respond more positively to it.

Second, God's people don't need to be surprised by change. They follow worship leaders who have credibility with the congregation. As you probably know, credibility is the product of integrity. A worship leader with integrity knows better than to surprise the congregation with a major change in the way the service is designed. Integrity will not allow them to live out the aphorism that it's easier to get forgiveness than permission. They know that surprising God's people with changes without warning may work for a while, but over the long haul it erodes the credibility of the worship leader with the people. Without credibility, you won't be able to minister to the people in your congregation and lead them in worship.

Third, God wants to work through worship leaders to lead His people toward spiritual maturity, and change is a necessary part of the growth process. For that reason, worship leaders have to keep in mind that teaching God's people and helping them to grow in worship may be a slow, arduous process, but it's worth the investment. Changes in worship, therefore, are not meant to marginalize segments of the congregation. Rather, they are intended to help God's people to grow spiritually as devoted disciples of Jesus Christ.

- How do you intend to nurture creativity as you develop worship services?
- Who for you is a good example of integrity for worship leaders?

Design the Service

In every week of a worship leader's life, the time will come for this crucial step to be taken. Usually the time will come before the worship leader's ready for it. A few more ideas still need to be developed for the service, and the organization of the service still needs to be tweaked, but time has run out. The plan must be finalized even though it feels as if the other steps have not been taken. The worship leader has no choice but to design the service. Sunday's coming, and the leader must be ready to lead God's people as they gather that day for worship.

That's a common struggle for ministers. Preachers rarely finish the work of preparing their Sunday sermons before they have to preach them. They have no other choice but to stop the preparation and get on with the delivery of the message they have prepared. They trust the work of the Holy Spirit to take their preparation and work a miracle in the lives of the people who listen to the sermon. Other worship leaders deal with the same struggle. They take the worship service they have planned, even though it's not really finished, and trust God to enhance it for His glory.

Because time is always in short supply, worship leaders do well to make the best use of their week. One of the best ways to capitalize on the time is to develop a weekly planning process. Since every church is different, the planning process will vary. Generally speaking, however, the process needs to include some basic deadlines such as when the theme will be determined, when the decision will be made about the elements to be used and the way they will be expressed in the service, and when the design has to be finalized.

You can save time in planning by keeping the design template in view. The template shows the flow of movement through the service even though some phases may be expanded while others may be diminished in any given service. By using the template, you will have a reliable pattern that should help you to expedite the planning process.

As stated previously, time can also be used more wisely if the pastor develops a sermon plan and shares it with the other worship leaders. Just think about the valuable time that can be saved for other worship leaders by knowing well in advance what the pastor intends to preach each Sunday. Music could be chosen in keeping with the sermon, rehearsals could be more purposeful, and the other worship leaders could sense the fulfillment that comes with knowing the role they played in worship helped the congregation to connect with the proclamation of God's Word in the sermon.

The point about a preaching plan has been made several times now, but repeating it in this context makes sense. As a time-saver and a tool for the stewardship of worship resources, a pastor owes it to the congregation to give serious attention to a sermon plan. On Monday, other worship leaders should be able to ask their pastor, the chief worship leader, about the sermon to be preached the following Sunday. They should be able to get an answer that gives them direction as they plan the service.

Along with the challenge of time constraints, worship leaders face the dilemma related to the announcements. In many churches, announcements are included in the most awkward and inappropriate places in the service. The same scenario is played all too often. The worship service begins, and God's people are drawn to Him by voicing their praise to Him through singing and praying. Then, in the middle of this pivotal phase of worship, someone stands at the pulpit to remind the congregation that the nominating committee will meet at 3 P.M., the goal for the special missions offering has not yet been reached, and the flowers on the offering table were provided by the Simpson family. Once the announcements have been shared, the service resumes as the people try to pick up where they left off in worship. Their attention has been shifted away from praising the Lord and diverted to matters that are certainly important, but not so vital that the worship service has to stop for the congregation to be reminded of them.

Instead of including the announcements in such an awkward spot in the service, consider two other possibilities. Either place them at the very beginning of the service as a means of assembling the people's minds and hearts for worship, or bring them up at the conclusion of the service. If you decide to place them at the beginning of the service, try to deal with them succinctly, and transition to the gathering song by way of a Scripture passage that calls God's people to worship. If you choose the end of the service, keep in mind that the attention span of the congregation may be short because everyone starts thinking about leaving the worship center. Make the transition to the closing congregational action in worship – praying, singing, or quoting a Bible passage together – as smoothly and quickly as possible.

Technology has helped congregations to deal effectively with the dilemma over announcements. Thanks to looping features installed in projection software, the announcements can be prepared in advance and shown one at a time in slow and steady increments. Depending on the number of announcements and the time devoted to running the projection system for them before and after the service, the people in the congregation can see the announcement enough to get the needed information. If you have that kind of technology available in your church and put it to work as suggested, you won't need as much time to talk through the announcements.

One more suggestion about announcements needs to be considered. When you prepare to share the announcements, try to talk about them in terms of opportunities for ministry. If the people hear them couched in those terms, they will grow to understand the connection between worship and service as two sides of the same coin. They will come that much closer to grasping worship as lifestyle as well as an event.

- What system will you use in the process of weekly worship planning?
- How will you handle the announcements in the worship services you design?

Prepare a Worship Guide

When people take a trip, they need a map to direct them to their destination. In the same way, God's people in worship need a guide to help them as they move through the service. The worship leaders know where the people will be going because they have planned the journey toward an encounter with God. If the people in the pews know something about what's ahead of them in worship, they can focus their minds and hearts on the encounter with God that awaits them. A printed worship guide gives them what they need to know as they worship.

A worship guide also functions as a teaching tool. Congregations need worship leaders not only to lead them in Sunday services but to disciple them in the way to an encounter with God individually as well as corporately. Worship leaders who want their congregations to be healthy expressions of the body of Christ give attention to teaching about worship even while they are planning and leading Sunday services. One teaching tool that works extremely well is a worship guide.

Why is a worship guide such a useful teaching tool? It shows God's people the phases of worship through which they will go in their meeting with Him. As they see the outline of the service – sometimes called the order of worship – provided in the guide, they can gain a better grasp of how worship involves movement. They will see that it's not a static experience. On the other hand, it's not like wandering lost in the forest without a sense of direction.

Learning the phases of movement in corporate worship will benefit God's people as they gather on Sunday. Likewise, it will have a positive influence on their personal worship experiences. The path they learn in public worship on Sunday can help them in their private encounters with Him during the week.

If you want to use the worship guide to be an effective teaching tool, consider the following suggestions. First, keep the outline of the service brief and clear. As a general rule, be suggestive rather than exhaustive in the layout of the service. Too much information about the service in the guide may distract the people. A general outline that presents the basic movement should be sufficient to show God's people where you are taking them in the service.

Second, take advantage of headings in the worship guide. For example, in the previous chapter the basic template was described under the following headings:

Assembling
Praising
Confessing
Focusing

Preaching
Inviting
Going

By placing these headings in the guide, you can show how the service goes from one phase to another.

Of course, other headings can be used. For example, Scripture passages like Isaiah 6:1-8 can serve well to provide some headings for the worship service outline:

I Saw the Lord
The Earth is Full of His Glory
My Eyes Have Seen the King
Then I Heard the Voice of the Lord
Here I Am. Send Me!

Simple headings like these can play a helpful role in showing God's people how to worship Him. For that reason, you will not regret incorporating them in the worship guide.

Third, include information in the worship guide about how to respond in the invitation time. The worship service will include seasoned believers who have known the Lord personally and have walked with Him for a long time. Also included in the service are new believers who need to know about obeying the Lord's command about baptism. People who don't know the Lord personally will be there too. Some of the people present will know about how to respond at the invitation as God's Spirit nudges them, but others won't have a clue. Someone will need to teach them. By describing in the worship guide how decisions can be registered, you can rest assured that you have done what's necessary as a worship leader to help them respond to the Lord as they encounter Him.

The culture of the congregation has to be considered when considering these suggestions. Adapting them to your particular ministry setting may be challenging, but accepting the challenge is part of your ministry as a worship leader.

- What are some other ways in which the worship guide can be used as a teaching tool?
- How can you adapt the suggestions for preparing a worship guide to your ministry setting?

Use a Wrap-Up Checklist

When the service has been designed in keeping with these recommended steps, take the time to add a vital finishing touch. Step back and take one last look at the worship experience you have planned. Five factors in particular deserve attention in this wrap-up phase of the planning process.

The Foundation Factor

The foundational goal of worship never changes. Corporate worship involves a community of believers who gather in order to meet God in a specific time and place. This gathering may look different from one week to another, but the one constant is God Himself. He meets His people in worship, and they respond to Him by acknowledging Him as Lord.

The foundational source of guidance in worship planning never changes either. The Bible – God's Word – must be considered as the authoritative guide for what we do in worship. Prescriptive passages like 1 Corinthians 12 delineate how orderly worship can be done in order to avoid chaos. Descriptive passages about worship also abound. The Bible is full of examples of believers at worship that shed light on the different elements of worship. Equally important, they reveal the heart of the believer who experiences true worship.

God promised us His Holy Spirit to guide and teach us. His Spirit dwells in us and helps us as we plan worship. The task is so big that we can't possibly do it on our own. We don't know enough by ourselves to plan services that could facilitate a congregation's encounter with God. Through an attitude of humility and prayer, we can approach the task confidently because of His presence as we plan and lead the service.

The Form Factor

The Bible validates certain elements to be used in worship, and worship leaders must decide which elements will be used in any given service. Making that decision is necessary because the proper arrangement of elements shapes the service so the congregation can focus on the primary goal of worship. Form also has an aesthetic value in that it provides cognitive and emotional progression through the service. For these reasons, worship leaders do well to make sure that the elements are arranged to create an environment in which life-transforming worship can take place.

One way to strengthen the stylistic integrity of a worship experience is to plan the service in keeping with a theme. Some worship services may be planned to be more theme-enhanced than theme-driven. In either case, the theme is an important organizing principle for designing worship services.

The Function Factor

Elements included in a worship service need to be presented to engage God's people in active participation. A particular element can be presented in a variety of ways. Take prayer for example. The congregation can be led to pray in the service if worship leaders plan the element with the intention of engaging the people in praying themselves. Another example is scripture reading. Think of the number of ways God's people can be led to worship through the reading of His Word if worship leaders would think of them as participants instead of spectators.

Along with the elements, the setting in which the worship service takes place has to be considered. The worship center itself has to be prepared for the service. The resources the congregation will use in worship need to be prepared and ready for the people as they arrive. Likewise, the musical resources have to be in place, and the technical equipment – lighting, sound, and projection systems – must be ready to go. Also, the people responsible for these functions must be ready for worship. They need to see themselves as worship leaders even though they may not lead the service from the platform. As worship leaders, they need to be spiritually prepared to play their part in leading God's people to encounter Him in the service.

The Focus Factor

The worship service should function in a way that allows the people in the congregation to focus their attention on God. Turning the minds and hearts of God's people toward Him means balancing the presentation of the elements. Too much of the same manner of presentation can render predictable, sterile worship services that don't have an effect on the worshipers at all. On the other hand, a worship leader can include too many modes of presentation in the same service that create a kind of circus effect. As a result, people are distracted from the real purpose of worship and focus their attention on the many modes of presentation.

The circus effect can happen when too many people plan the worship service and when no coordinating person or principle is there to guide the design. When a need exists every Sunday to platform each of the ministries of the church, promote all of the projects undertaken by the congregation, and provide time for other acts of worship, a circus effect is likely to characterize the service. Such an effect can happen in any congregation, and the culprit is always the same: a lack of coordination.

The worship leaders themselves must also take a long, hard look at themselves as platform leaders. Their role is to help God's people to meet Him in the corporate worship experience. Worship leaders can design services that are too platform-oriented. Although unintentional, they make the platform the center of the worship activity. God's people look on passively in their pews, much more like an audience watching a production than a congregation gathering to focus their minds and hearts on God. Granted, moving the center of activity to the pews may take a paradigm shift, but it's worth the effort if it results in God's people turning to Him in worship.

The Freedom Factor

Although worship leaders are tasked with the responsibility for planning worship services, they generally don't have the freedom to do whatever they want. The culture of the congregation restricts them as they design the services. Churches in which a liturgy is used in worship are restricted by the liturgical calendar and by church-wide or denomination-wide parameters set in keeping with the doctrinal confessions or creeds.

Congregations that don't use a standard liturgy in worship may not face the same restriction. They don't have to follow the calendar of the church year in worship planning. They are free to choose those themes which seem important in the life of the church at the time. However, restrictions still exist in the culture of the congregation. Worship leaders do well to understand the culture as a part of the worship planning process. If they do, they will be able to interpret the prevailing attitudes regarding key worship issues. For example, they will know their congregations' attitude toward the range of physical postures that can be used comfortably in worship. Furthermore, they will know how to lead the congregation to incorporate expressions that will reflect the freedom in worship affirmed in the Scriptures.

Surrender Your Plan to God

As you have seen, designing a worship service takes a great deal of effort. Once you design it, however, you need to take one last step. You must take what you have done in planning and surrender it to the Lord to be used in the worship service in whatever way He chooses. Surrendering your work to Him means that you hold on to what He directs you to keep, and you let go of what He doesn't want you to retain. Sometimes you get an impression from Him early in the process, but sometimes you won't know until the dynamic moment when you are actually leading the service.

As you surrender the plan to Him, ask Him to use it for His glory. And trust Him to work in miraculous ways as you lead His people to encounter Him. If you do, you won't be disappointed.

- How much time each should be given to working through this checklist?
- What other factors should be added to the checklist?

CHAPTER 4

Expressing Worship:
How Do We Offer It?

The decade of the nineties will undoubtedly go down in history as a time of great upheaval and heated debate within many churches regarding issues of style in worship. This phenomenon, observed across most Christian denominations, spawned a plethora of books on the subject.[6] Though differing in their approach and perspective, all of these publications have one theme in common: the worship of God is expressed by human beings, and therefore the various acts of worship are related to a human (or *cultural*) context.

The discussion concerning which particular expressions of worship are acceptable and which are not has been going on for a long time. The offerings brought by the brothers Cain and Abel (Gen. 4:3-5), David's exuberant dance of joy before the Lord when the ark was brought to Jerusalem (2 Sam. 6:12-23), and the anointing of Jesus' feet by Mary in Bethany (John 12:-1-8) all precipitated a disagreement of some sort – one of which ended with a murder!

In the early days of the New Testament church, worship expression was not free of dissention either. In the Corinthian church, the Lord's Supper was shared in conjunction with a church-wide *Agape* feast. Apparently those worship celebrations had gotten out of hand in Corinth. Some believers were enjoying the expression of their worship so much that they had missed the point of it all – remembering the death of their Savior Jesus Christ! Paul chastised the congregation for abusing the Lord's Supper (1 Cor. 11:20-22). Eventually the custom of celebrating an *Agape* feast as an adjunct to the Lord's Supper was dropped.

After the emperor Constantine was converted to Christianity in 312 A.D., Christians enjoyed the status of mainstream religion. Three main liturgical traditions of worship emerged – each reflected its own corporate style of expression: the Eastern liturgy in Constantinople, the Gallican liturgy in Europe, and the Roman liturgy in Rome. Worship expression in the Eastern liturgy was highly influenced by the Hellenistic value for aesthetic beauty. Basically, this value translated into the use of elaborate ceremony for worship in a highly artistic environment. In contrast, worship practice in Rome was characterized by simplicity and less ceremony. It reflected the pragmatism of its culture with a simple, yet majestic liturgy. The Gallican liturgy was more dramatic and colorful in expression than the Roman liturgy. It included a greater use of symbolism and was a longer, more flexible version.[7]

The development of liturgies throughout the medieval years brought both form and expression in worship under strict control of governing church councils. The worship expression of the congregation became increasingly passive as professional church leaders performed the sacred drama. Latin, the official language of the liturgy, was not understood by the vast majority of worshipers, and the expression of singing was relegated to official choirs or professional cantors.

During the sixteenth century, the Protestant Reformation provided an opportunity to express worship once again in more personal ways. Though worship expression was diverse throughout the churches of Europe, the services were offered in the vernacular of the worshipers, and singing once more became a congregational expression.

As the story of Christian worship has continued into the twenty-first century, the worldwide expansion of the church has brought with it indigenous expressions of worship as varied as the cultures in which the gospel has found a home. Although the *story* is the same, the methods of proclaiming the truth of Christ and praising God for His grace are as multi-faceted as the people whom God has redeemed.

The Content and Context of Worship

The expression of worship in a congregational setting never occurs in a vacuum. To have meaning, it must be attached to a given cultural context. That is precisely why issues of expression have sparked such heated debate through the years. On one hand, some will argue against "newer" expressions because those expressions are not perceived by some as belonging to the context (as defined by the keepers of a particular tradition). On the other hand, older expressions may be attacked out of a sense that they do not authentically relate to today's society. Both perspectives are framed by a given context – either an *established tradition* or a *contemporary culture*, hence the labels often given to worship services as "traditional" or "contemporary."[8]

In reality, the debate often stems from confusion over the *content* of worship as opposed to its *context*. The content of Christian worship is comprised of a re-telling and celebration of the gospel. It is the basis for our gathering as a community of the redeemed. As such, it is non-negotiable and timeless. We worship the same Lord Jesus as the apostles did two thousand years before us. Yet, contextualizing the unchanging truth of the gospel takes on different indigenous forms, and thus our worship expressions will necessarily be many and varied.

Problems with worship expression occur when what began simply as an expression subtly shifts over time to take on a life of its own. At that point, the worshiper no longer views an expression as simply that, but subconsciously equates the expression with the validity of the worship experience. In other words, an absence of the expression is perceived as an absence of "real worship" in the mind of the worshiper. Thus, the content of worship is confused with its context.

Some aspects of culture may provide suitable and meaningful expressions of the content of Christian worship. Some of these may be cross-cultural while others may be unique to a certain group of people. Because different cultural contexts exist, any discussion of worship expression must take place in reference to these contexts in order to understand their meaning to the worshiper. In a larger sense, Christian expression itself was grounded in the context of Judaism. Certain traditional aspects were retained unchanged (the importance of faith for example), while other aspects were reinterpreted in the new context. An example of the latter, the unleavened bread and wine of the Jewish Passover became central to Christians as symbols of the atoning work of Christ through the crucifixion, representing His broken body and His shed blood for the remission of sin.

Much of the confusion in worship seems to stem from a lack of understanding regarding worship expression. How can leaders help their congregations to sort through some of these worship issues and find healthy ways of expressing heartfelt worship? As church leaders, we need criteria for helping our congregations authentically express their worship. The following ten principles encourage our congregations to express themselves authentically in worship.

1. Worship Requires an Attitude of Recognizing God as God (Ps. 95:6-7)

Sometimes we get derailed in our understanding of what it is we are doing when we engage in corporate worship. The Old Testament word *shachah*, translated "worship," means *to bow down*. Likewise, a principal New Testament word for worship, occurring sixty times, is the Greek *proskuneo*, which means to "kiss the hand" (out of respect), or "to kneel or prostrate oneself before another in order to express respect." At its heart, worship is an attitude of submission and an act of bowing oneself before the Almighty.

Controversial issues regarding worship expression seem to lose ground when placed against the backdrop of personal and corporate submission to God. As individual autonomy and preference fade in the light of God's sovereignty and glory, so does the notion that worship exists for the benefit and pleasure of the worshiper. While it is true that worship does benefit us, we miss the point if we think of the benefits as the real purpose. Genuine worship begins with a right understanding of our relationship with God: He is our Creator, and we are His creation. As such, our appropriate expression is characterized by bowing our will, our minds, and our hearts before God. Worship is expressed by believers, but it is *for* God.

This truth provides a much-needed perspective. When a congregation truly understands this foundation, expression issues will necessarily diminish, and expression will be seen for what it is: a natural outpouring of the human soul bowing before its Creator.

2. Worship Requires a Pure and Sincere Heart (Heb. 10:22)

It seems incredible to think that one might try to draw near to God with an insincere heart! How could we think that He wouldn't notice? Or that He wouldn't care? But strangely enough, many who attend worship gatherings Sunday after Sunday might be described by the phrase "the lights are on—but nobody's home!" Physically awake and alert, these would-be worshipers are able to go through the Sunday motions; they know the drill. But they haven't connected with the Almighty in worship. Simply put, they are *disengaged*.

It happens every time an individual sits through a worship event and glibly goes through the worship routines (standing, sitting, reading, singing, and listening) without making the connection of what he or she is doing. Half-hearted or token participation in a worship service without a vital heart connection is fruitless. A sincere heart connection plays a critical role in the authenticity of the worship experience.

Leaders need to be reminding their churches of this truth, or subconsciously some would-be worshipers may continue to think that worship is only about showing up at gatherings, having nothing to do with the state of our hearts. Read on for a related truth.

3. Religious Acts Do Not Necessarily Mean Worship (Isa. 1:11a)

A major task for worship leaders is helping congregations to fully engage with God in corporate worship. Perhaps chief among the many obstacles to this goal is a faulty understanding of the nature of worship. Many church-goers settle for a check-list-driven worship experience in which showing up, sitting up, staying up (at least half-awake!), and checking off each line item on the worship guide are enough to meet the weekly obligations of worship. To some who attend worship gatherings, "going to church" is all that matters, regardless of any personal investment beyond attendance. This legalistic attitude misses the point. It cheapens the concept of real worship just as it ignores all aspects of the relationship between the Redeemer and the redeemed who would worship Him as Savior and Lord.

Isaiah brought the Lord's indictment against the people of Judah for their presumption that the outward ritual (worship expression) had no connection to inward righteousness. The prophet declared that the multitude of their sacrifices, the incense, the religious festivals and feasts, and their prayers would be rejected by the Lord because they were carried out hypocritically and with sinful hearts. Not only were such activities unacceptable, but Isaiah declared that they were a burden to the Lord (Isa. 1:11-15). Somehow the would-be worshipers had forgotten that worship actions, in and of themselves, were never pleasing to God. They would only be meaningful and acceptable to Him if offered with a life that honored Him.

So, how should worship leaders approach this discipleship challenge? It is primarily a ministry task in which leaders continuously encourage their people, through personal example and public teaching, to connect worship to discipleship. The expression of corporate worship can then become an overflow of the individual worship that is taking place in the believer's heart throughout the week. We must teach that the authentic worship of God is a heartfelt response to God's incredible grace and mercy poured out on our lives. This expression will never lose its authenticity as long as an awareness of God's grace and mercy is prominent in our hearts and minds. On the other hand, it can never be authentic if the worship actions on Sunday are divorced from a lifestyle of worship.

Worship leaders would do well to remember that, ultimately, only the Holy Spirit can enliven a heart to genuinely worship God. We can and should teach that going through the motions of worship is not a valid expression. Clocking time in the pew will never substitute for engaging with God in worship.

4. God's Word Is the Authority for Worship--Not Our Traditions (Mark 7:6b-7)

Human nature makes us fond of tradition. Traditions are found in practically every context of our lives – community, school, holidays, family, and of course, church. Traditions are simply reenactments of events which possess some type of symbolic meaning. For example, serving a turkey for dinner on Thanksgiving is a tradition which reminds Americans of what the New England colonists ate as they shared that first thanksgiving meal with the Wampanoag Indians in 1621.

Traditions are not bad. The truth is they are simply tools which provide a way to help people process what is important to them. They can help us remember and celebrate important relationships, beliefs, and events. Regardless of the setting, traditions can be found throughout the contexts of worship. Some of these are based on Scripture, such as the celebration of the Lord's Supper. Others have grown out of past meaningful expressions. Holding "Fifth Sunday Singings" followed by a church social is not mentioned in the Bible, but it is an example of a particular tradition which some churches have found encouraging in the past. The tradition is neither right nor wrong. It is simply a *tradition* which has helped certain church fellowships to worship in a different and meaningful way. Other indigenous Christian worship traditions can be found around the world.

An order of worship can be thought of as a tradition. As was stated in a previous chapter, worship planners in evangelical churches have more freedom in organizing the worship service than do liturgical churches. But even without a fixed liturgy the worship service format can become a predictable template that is used without much variation from week to week. Used in this way, the order of worship can become a tradition. Worship leaders need to be aware of the powerful effect certain traditions can have on individuals. It may not be such a surprise then that altering the placement of the offertory in the order of worship would seem strange to some worshipers who are accustomed to the prior format. Some churches, for example, place the offertory immediately preceding the sermon while others do this at the conclusion of the service. Either placement can be effective. Should worship leaders steer away from making the change since some may be uncomfortable if you change it? No. The answer will depend on what may provide the most effective way to lead people in worship. Sometimes it calls for prayerfully shifting the traditions.

Do only "traditional" churches express traditions? Interestingly, most churches, traditional or otherwise, enact new traditions at the point at which they decide to do anything over time in a repeated sequence. A church may plan a successful ministry event, and then repeat it again later, and in the course of time, voilá! They have a new tradition! Even a "non-traditional" church may decide to celebrate their anniversary each year, thus forming a new tradition!

In the context of worship practice, leaders need to be aware that two dangers exist regarding traditions. The first lies in the possibility of placing cultural traditions of the church on equal footing with biblical traditions. Jesus indicted the Pharisees for elevating their customs while ignoring the Word of God (Mark 7:8). We must be careful how we view worship traditions today as well. The order of worship, the choice of songs, the use of choir robes (or not), or the use of particular musical instruments, to name a few, must be considered as "traditions of men" and not as holy writ. However helpful it may be, no manmade tradition should be exalted to the place of Scripture. A tradition is a vehicle – a tool which can help us express our worship.

It is possible that a particular tradition could lose its meaning. In such cases it is also possible that the tradition itself might not be thought of as a tool pointing to something beyond itself, but as a sacred entity in itself. When meaningful traditions become "sacred cows," there is a human resistance to change or discard them for fear that, in doing so, an essential part of the faith is being compromised or surrendered. When traditions become more than just traditions, essentially they have become non-negotiable parts of the content, not just tools for engaging our worship. The same is true of symbols or icons. A crucifix is a visible pointer to the sacrificial death of our Lord Jesus. But when the article is thought to possess an attribute *in and of itself* such as a talisman for protection, the object has taken on more than symbolic reality. We must guard against unwittingly allowing our traditions to become our new idols.

The second danger is the potential for a particular tradition to lose its original meaning. Whenever this happens, its continued practice may become nothing more than an empty action, perhaps thought of as fulfilling a religious responsibility without any thought to the relationship God desires with His children. For this reason, it is important that worship leaders take the time to help members of the congregation understand why they do what they do in corporate worship.

What things are essential according to God's Word? What do we practice in worship that might be considered our human traditions? How well do these traditions point us to the *essentials* of worship and help us to authentically express our worship? For worship leaders, these are tough questions worth exploring.

5. God is the Sole Audience of Worship (Matt. 6:1)

The phrase "An Audience of One" has been used as the theme of worship recordings, book projects, and worship ministry statements in recent days. The concept helps us focus on the fact that our corporate and individual worship actions should be directed toward God. It would seem that any visible expression in the context of corporate worship could potentially serve three different interests: self, others, or God. If we do what we do primarily because it is of some personal benefit, then we are serving ourselves. If we do what we do with the secret hope of impressing others, again, we are seeing those around us as our audience. However, if we do what we do in worship out of a sincere desire to express our worship to God, then we are considering Him as our "audience."

Many books on worship reference the analogy of worship provided by the nineteenth-century theologian Søren Kierkegaard. In it he compares corporate worship to a drama. A faulty view would see the congregation as the "audience" and the platform personalities (leaders) as the "actors." Kierkegaard taught that members of the congregation are the actors; the platform leaders are prompters; and God is the only true audience in worship.[9]

How did the Church ever arrive at the conclusion that corporate worship was something to be watched from the pew? Even though that concept is nowhere to be found in the Bible, many churchgoers have adopted that mentality – and the corresponding point of view – that all the worship "action" happens on the platform. Is it any wonder that worship attendees make departing comments much like those heard as they exit a secular concert or show? *"I enjoyed that today!" "The music was great!"* or perhaps, *"I didn't like the worship today very much."* Platform-driven action which does not seek to actively engage the people in the pew fails to educate the church as to the personal responsibility of worship. The work of worship belongs to the congregation!

Jesus warned that some false worshipers were expressing themselves for another audience – namely the people around them who might observe their pious expressions. He referred to three religious activities – giving alms to the poor, prayer, and fasting – in which the Pharisees engaged. In each case, Jesus exposed their worship expression as self-seeking and thus, inauthentic (Matt. 6:1-18).

6. Worship Is Active Engagement with God (Ps. 95:1-2).

Note the active verbs mentioned in the Scripture passage: Come – sing – shout – extol. These are verbs which call for action in worship. While intercessory prayer exists, humanly speaking *intercessory worship* is not possible. Since the activity of worship is predicated upon a personal relationship with God through Christ, the activity of worship is a personal one, even within the context of corporate worship.

Many churches refer to the worship center as the "auditorium." The word comes from the Latin *audire*, "to hear." The term "auditorium" emphasizes a certain degree of passivity in worship as taking place in the "hearing place." Not to diminish the need for worshipers to hear the Word of God preached in worship, here is, however, the need for more active responses as well. The following principle will provide more suggestions on how that might occur.

7. The Bible Endorses a Wide Variety of Worship Expression (Ps. 150:6)

You only need to read the Psalms to find a wide variety of human expression in worship. Appropriate expressions include various postures, gestures, and verbal expressions, as well as musical and emotional expressions.

Postures mentioned in the Bible include standing, kneeling and bowing, lifting of hands, and being still before the Lord. The psalmist also refers to various gestures, including clapping of hands, dancing, jumping and processional. Examples of verbal expressions include shouting, singing, and speaking. Various emotional expressions in worship found in the Bible include laughter, tears, grief, joy, and awe. Jesus' even expressed the emotion of holy indignation on one occasion as He sought to bring glory to His Heavenly Father (John 2:13-16).

It is interesting to note that the various expressions mentioned here were found in the course of everyday life as well. The Hebrew people were an expressive people, and it was only natural that their characteristic expressivity would be present in times of worship. They sang, they danced, they laughed and cried, they grieved and rejoiced. All of these expressions were a part of everyday life. In their worship, these active expressions were directed toward their God.

Physical expression in worship seems to be a point of contention within some churches today. There is a need for a great deal of education regarding what the Bible says about it. This could potentially unlock some of the self-imposed restrictions that certain segments of the American church have placed upon themselves. For example, some see the raising of hands as a charismatic practice in worship. On the contrary, it is a biblical posture mentioned in both Old and New Testaments. In fact, one of the Hebrew words for praise, *yadah*, means "to extend the hands in praise or thanksgiving." It is used 114 times in the Old Testament.[10] Although the Psalms were not written as prescriptions for worship, they certainly provide some descriptions of how God's people worshiped Him. Some American congregations are quite expressive in their worship practice because of their ethnic and cultural composition.

Musical Expression: the Church's Song

As mentioned earlier, music can be considered as an element of worship. By its very nature, however, it can be considered a manner of expression in worship. Music has been an important aspect of worship from earliest times. Sadly, in our day, it has also become a point of great friction and division within church fellowships.[11]

The first song in the Bible was sung by Miriam and Moses in praise to God for delivering His people from the Egyptians (Ex. 15:1-18). Some other examples of biblical songs of praise include the song of Deborah (Judg. 5:1-31), and the song of Hanna after dedicating Samuel to God (1 Sam. 2:1-10). The Book of Psalms in the Old Testament is a compilation "hymnbook" of the Hebrew people, although the songs were passed down in an oral tradition. The different psalms come from many different time periods of Jewish history. They include songs of praise, petition, thanksgiving, and even lament.

Two distinct musical traditions existed in the Old Testament. The first was music that was spontaneous and ecstatic, or music that was expected to usher the worshiper into a supernatural experience with God (for an example see 1 Sam. 10:5-6). The second tradition was the music used in the temple. This music was more formal and was performed by the highly trained temple musicians (1 Chron. 15:16). In the account of the dedication of the temple, God's presence was revealed through musical performance (2 Chron. 5:11-14).

In the early church, worship was no longer the work of a trained priesthood – but rather the work of the congregation. The church seemed to have completely abandoned the professionalism of both the temple and the synagogue.

We also know that Jesus and His disciples sang a hymn at the conclusion of the celebration of the Passover in the Upper Room (Mark 14:26), indicating that song was a natural part of their informal gatherings. Paul wrote about singing in worship to the churches at Corinth (1 Cor. 14:26) and Ephesus (Eph. 5:19).

In his letter to the Colossians, Paul mentioned three types of songs: psalms, hymns, and spiritual songs (Col 3:16). Although scholars really don't know for sure, the psalms were probably all the psalms and canticles common to Jewish worship (from the tabernacle, temple, synagogue). Hymns could have been newer expressions in song based on patterns of classical Greek poetry, such as the hymns to Christ, or *carmina Christi*. Examples of hymns can be found in Philippians 2:5-11, 1 Timothy 3:16, and 2 Timothy 2:11-13. The spiritual songs most likely consisted of wordless, improvised musical expressions that were called *pneumatic odes* or "songs upon the breath."

Some examples of biblical songs of praise in the New Testament include Mary's psalm of praise after being visited by the angel, sometimes referred to as the *Magnificat* from the Latin for "magnify" (Luke 1:46-55), Zechariah's psalm of praise, called the *Benedictus* from the Latin for "blessed" (Luke 1:67-79), and the *Gloria in excelsis Deo* of the angels (Luke 2:14). Even the last book of the Bible includes songs that will be sung in heaven to the Creator (Rev. 4:8, 11) and to the Risen Lamb (Rev. 5:11-14). Song obviously has played an important role in the worship expression of God's people from the beginning and will continue even throughout eternity!

Musical Expression: Instruments in Worship

The use of musical instruments in worship can be easily traced back to the Old Testament. Psalm 150 is a compendium of the types of instruments which might have been played in the temple and on other occasions of worship. Typical instruments included the shofar (ram's horn), silver trumpet, lyre, harp, oboe, flute, drums and cymbals. Today, the use of instruments in worship has been a source of controversy. During the Patristic era and again during the

Calvinist Reformation, instruments in worship were disallowed. The argument against their usage came from the perception that music for worship was *logocentric* (or word-based). Some of the strongest objections to instruments during the Patristic era were in response to how instruments were associated with pagan culture. During the Reformation some centuries later, Calvin's position in support of unison, unaccompanied congregational singing was determined by his belief that singing was a community-oriented expression of worship and that instrumental music – without words – served no purpose in worship. Congregational singing under Calvin's influence consisted of singing from the Book of Psalms in French in a metrical paraphrase format.[12]

At times throughout the church's history the organ, handbells, piano, and various other instruments have been used effectively to help worshipers express their musical praise. In the twenty-first century, acoustic and electric guitars, electronic keyboards, synthesizers, and percussion instruments have become an integral part of the soundscape for worship in many churches. Around the globe Christian musicians are using instruments indigenous to their cultures to give expression to their praise. The question is not so much which instruments to use, but how they can be used effectively in corporate worship. A general assumption regarding the role of instruments is that they should be used to *support* the singing. When the instrumental accompaniment masks the comprehension of the text, the use of instruments has overstepped an important boundary. Words in worship must always take priority over music.

Can instruments be used without words? In the Old Testament, instrumental music filled a prophetic role. Prophesying was at times accompanied by the playing of instruments. David would play the harp for King Saul and this would ease Saul's spiritual malady (1 Sam. 16:23).

In contemporary society, perhaps instruments may be used most effectively when they are playing a melody which has an association with a particular text. This approach will allow worshipers to focus their attention on a specific thought. Musical worship leaders must bear in mind that our purpose in using music in worship is *always* to point people to Christ and to help them engage with God, not to simply enjoy a good musical presentation.

Although music is an effective tool in worship, it is not the essence of worship. It is very possible (albeit uncommon) to experience corporate worship without a single note of music being played or sung. The fact that we have, in some way, come to depend on music so much in services may signal our need to reevaluate what its real purpose is in worship. It has the potential of being used as a vehicle for both thought and emotion in ways which can direct our attention to God.

8. Corporate Worship Should Build Up the Body of Christ (1 Cor. 14:26)

A disturbing trend can be noticed in certain quarters of the American Church today. It's the elevation of the individual over the corporate in worship. It is not a new problem in the church as evidenced by Paul in his first letter to the Corinthians.

In his epistle, Paul rebuked the church for the spirit of self-indulgence demonstrated by their worship practices. When it came to celebrating the Lord's Table, instead of exhibiting a spirit of community, each individual would partake of the Lord's Supper without waiting on others to arrive. Some would overindulge and leave late-comers with little or nothing to eat.

Spiritual gifts, likewise, were not expressed for the benefit of the assembly, but they were exercised in an unrestrained fashion for personal edification. Apparently, for the Corinthian Christian, personal satisfaction (read *gratification*) was the rule of the day. No attention was given to the edification of the congregation as a whole. To our twenty-first century ears, that description sounds far too familiar!

Paul rebuked the Corinthian believers with a reminder that whatever was offered in the context of corporate worship – a hymn, or a word of instruction, a revelation, a tongue or an interpretation - had to be given *for the building up of the church* (1 Cor. 14:26). Paul's rebuke meant that the various personal expressions of worship in the corporate context were to be subject to the principle of corporate edification.

9. *Love for Others Is an Important Component of Worship Expression (1 Cor. 13:1)*

In 1 Corinthians 13:1, Paul reminds us that eloquence without love makes us sound like nothing more than a clanging gong or a clashing cymbal. We would be all sound but no substance. Notice what Paul's comment says about worship expression. Do you think that it's actually possible to give verbal expressions of praise and yet be unloving to those around us? Paul notes that the result is just noise, not music to the ears of our Heavenly Father.

Corporate worship brings together the twin relationships referred to as the Great Commandments: loving God and loving others as you love yourself (Luke 10:27). The ability of one to worship with authenticity is directly related to the personal relationship one has with God as well as his or her relationships with others in the congregation. A broken relationship in either direction creates serious obstacles in the pursuit of transformative worship.

On the subject of love, Paul reminded the Corinthians that everything God created could be considered permissible, but everything permitted may not be beneficial or constructive. For that reason Christians had to do what was best for others (1 Cor. 10:23-24). The context for Paul's instruction was the common practice by some Christians of eating meat that had been previously offered as a sacrifice to pagan idols. Not that they had offered the meat to idols, but it had been purchased from sources which had ties to such practices, and they knew it. Paul gave license for Christians to partake truly of the meat in question. But with the liberty came the important responsibility of loving others. If weaker Christians could not partake of this meat without harming their consciences, the more mature believers would then be obligated to keep a weaker Christian from falling spiritually. Personal conviction might not change on the issue, but the more mature believer would accommodate his or her behavior out of love for the more sensitive Christians. Paul gave the bottom line: the responsibility of love should supersede the privilege of liberty.

Worship contexts can potentially create similar scenarios. Certain practices of worship expression might be acceptable to some while creating stumbling blocks to others. One example is the use of indigenous musical styles as a part of the worship experience.[13] Some worshipers may feel a great sense of freedom in worshiping God through a musical style popular within a specific culture. But what if that same musical style is associated with a degenerate lifestyle in the mind of a new believer in that culture? For one who may have come out of such a lifestyle, the idea of worshiping God with the same soundtrack might pose serious conflicts for the new believer. The apostle shows us how to nurture sensitivity to the spiritual needs of other Christians.

Paul's instruction is clear. What is permissible for some might not be in the best interest of the congregation. Worship leaders must know their culture, their people, and depend mightily on the Holy Spirit for discernment concerning these expression matters. In all instances, the rule of love should be applied.

10. Worship Is More Than an Event— It Is a Lifestyle (Rom. 12:1)

According to Paul's instructions in Romans 12:1, living a holy life for God is a worship expression. Ask many current churchgoers today about the idea of worship, and many of them will respond that it is an activity they *attend* once a week (usually Sundays) during which they sing some religious songs and listen to a sermon. The problem lies in the fact that many church attendees do not make worship a daily part of their lives. They limit worship to an occasional Sunday activity.

The New Testament does not allow us to compartmentalize worship in that way. Rather, the Scriptures teach us that worship is a holistic expression of our lives before God. Paul's writings emphasized that point when he instructed believers to consider everything they said and did as an act of worship in which they expressed gratitude to God through Christ the Lord (Col. 3:17).

What can we do as leaders to help worship have a more holistic perspective? We have an enormous responsibility to disciple our people in understanding the whole-life privilege of worship. Discipling congregations to truly experience worship – not from a "got to" perspective which fulfills the obligatory weekly trek to church, but from a "get to" attitude which desires to honor God – is leadership's big challenge. Meeting it will require an unending amount of effort in teaching what real worship is and what drives it. We need to foster that idea and resource the families in our congregation to find ways to do this at home.

- When was the last time you led a Bible study on appropriate expressions for worship?
- Which of the ten principles regarding worship expression causes you the most difficulty?

CHAPTER 5

Transitioning Worship:
How Do We Rethink It?

Change and the Local Church

We live in a time of relentless and on-going change. Just in the realm of technology alone change is broad and far-reaching. In fact, many of the technological products we purchase are replaced by newer and better versions often before we have finished paying for them. Various media outlets constantly remind us of our changing environment along with the underlying call for ever-newer and better ways of living. The concurrent shifts from an industrial to an information-driven society, from modernity to post-modernity mindsets, and from rural to global economies are just a few of the factors which define our world today. Perhaps Bob Dylan said it best in his song: *The times they are a-changin'*.[14]

Practically every church leader alive today has dealt with the effects of a changing culture upon the local church. As churches in America have found themselves increasingly surrounded by communities of non-churchgoers, and as many churchgoers themselves have called for leadership to be more in tune with the culture, the question of worship and cultural relevance has come to the forefront. Many leaders have struggled with how-to issues, such as: how to maintain a balance between the old and the new in worship; how to share the "old, old story" with a target group increasingly polarized by modern/postmodern ways of thinking;

how to incorporate new musical idioms and technological tools into corporate worship; and how to keep everyone happy! More than a few leaders have suffered forced terminations over issues related to changing worship styles.

Although the broad issue of cultural relevance relates to many aspects of church life, the discussion here will be limited to its relationship to corporate worship.

Why Should the Church Change?

This is a perfectly legitimate question and one that deserves a well-reasoned response. Unfortunately, some churches are implementing changes in their own worship environments without ever asking the question as to why. They are doing so because they are being swept along by what they see other "successful" churches doing or what the latest books tell them they should be doing, without an understanding of why certain changes should be undertaken.

In order to answer the question of why the church should change regarding worship, it needs to be expanded to *two* questions: First, *what* is changeable and what is not? And second, *why* (for what purpose) should those changeable aspects be altered?

What is Changeable, and What is Not?

It is not an understatement to say that, in its 2000-plus years of existence, the church has undergone change in many ways. It has spread from Jerusalem, to Judea, to Samaria and literally to the uttermost parts of the earth. Wherever it has gone, the church has carried the same gospel. That message has not changed. But, with its unchanging message of hope and life, the church has adapted remarkably to the cultures in which it has flourished. Whenever the church has been faithful in presenting the gospel and doctrines of the faith without compromise, people of differing cultures have often responded and expressed their faith in worship in their own indigenous forms. But whenever the message has been compromised, or perhaps conformed to pagan beliefs, the results have been syncretistic and erroneous, even though perhaps indigenous.

In order to arrive at a conclusion of what is changeable and what is not regarding worship, we must understand the distinction between style and substance. The substance of worship – the truth of the gospel, the teachings of God's Word, and the elements mentioned in Chapter 2 – will *transcend* culture. To the extent that cultural characteristics are not in conflict with biblical principles, the way corporate worship is implemented should *reflect* the culture – regarding its temperament, language, and other indigenous aspects.[15]

Although an unchanging substance of worship (or content) exists, the meaningful interaction of a people with that substance occurs at a cultural level. This involves factors of language, style, informational processing preferences, and other indigenous components. The factors which shape the cognitive and affective domains of a group of people as a whole will also influence how that group approaches the activity of corporate worship. These factors aid worshipers in making the content of the gospel meaningful to them. The linguistic vernacular, the musical styles, and the formality/informality of the worship environment are examples of some factors which may facilitate the worshiper's process of identifying and interacting with the content of worship. The basic underlying assumption is that genuine worship is conceivable in a wide variety of forms. These forms have the potential to carry the truth of the gospel through indigenous expressions of worship in ways that make sense to the various cultures around the globe. In other words, worship needs to be contextualized.

For What Purpose Should Change Be Implemented in Worship?

But what happens when cultural shifts take place? These changing cultural contexts provide the primary impetus for change in worship style within a given congregation. Leonard Sweet has identified four cultural shifts which are currently taking place in American culture: the shift from rational to experiential, from representative to participatory, from word-based to image-driven, and from individual to communal.[16] The four major areas which Sweet has described are having a tremendous impact upon current-day worship practices in America.

Emphasis on Experience of Worship

Consider the seating arrangement of many long-established congregations. Row after row of straight pews are neatly lined up, ready to provide a place for those who would enter the "auditorium" (literally *hearing place*) to listen to the "main event" of a worship service, which in their minds is the sermon. In such churches, worship appears to be an auditory experience – listening to the announcements, hearing musical presentations, and paying attention to a sermon. The worship is very programmatic. Yet some churchgoers in today's culture are growing discontent with the role of mere listener. They don't want simply to hear a sermon, they want to experience God. The description "worship experience" in place of "worship service" resonates with them. For them, worship means more than a "program." It is something to be experienced.

That reality should generate some questions for worship planners and leaders. Is what we are currently doing helping people to experience God? Does the corporate worship gathering require just listening, or does it call for engaging the mind and heart in recognizing and responding to God? Has enough attention been given to creating a healthy, inviting environment for people to worship God? Are there distractions in the environment which can be corrected if given proper attention? These and other questions can help leaders address the experiential component of worship.

Emphasis on personal participation

In recent years television program producers have allowed for a higher level of interaction on the part of viewers. Using technology as a sidekick to television programming, entertainment media have allowed television viewing audiences to interact with the content of their programs on-line. On *American Idol*, for example, viewers have the opportunity to text-message a vote for their favorite contestant, which significantly affects the outcome of the show. The *Wheel of Fortune* television game show encourages at-home viewers to log-on to their website and get a personal "spin I.D." which gives them a chance to win the same prize a contestant on the show receives. These examples, among others, point to a growing trend of personal interaction among those who were once part of a passive television viewing audience. Enter the new paradigm: couch potatoes can now personally participate via internet with the shows they watch on television!

The move beyond passive observer to active participant is actually healthy in regard to corporate worship. For too long, many churchgoers have clocked time in the pew "watching the show" and thinking that their physical presence was all that was required of them in worship. Even though a viewer mentality which focuses on the show up-front is still the expectation for some, a growing number of people desire to actively participate in worship. That's a move in the right direction!

Many churchgoers may not have read his book, but Robert Webber's description of worship as a verb would resonate powerfully with them.[17] A participatory culture seeks involvement, which includes worship as well. The emphasis on participation accounts for the kinesthetic worship forms evident in many churches today. Raised hands, rhythmic music, clapping with the songs, standing for extended periods of time while singing, and taking notes (fill-in-the-blank style) during the sermon are a few examples of increased hands-on participation in worship. Contemporary worshipers don't want to be spectators, nor do they want to be manipulated. But they do want to be involved.

As worship planners we need to find more ways to involve the congregation in active expression. We should examine the frequency and variety of congregational worship actions and assess how we are doing in leadership at that point.

Emphasis on the visual

Our culture is filled with screens. They are everywhere in increasing numbers. From banks to restaurants, to animated billboards, to portable DVD players installed in vehicles, to cell phones and digital music players with video, screens are integrated into the daily lives of Americans, young and old alike. In worship, the proliferation of projection screens, along with other visual elements, has enhanced the worshipers' sensory interaction during corporate worship. According to Barna, more than six out of ten Protestant evangelical churches use projection screen technology in their worship.[18] Among smaller churches, 47 percent of them use this type of technology. Many churches are also using cameras to allow worshipers to see the platform leaders on the screens during worship services.

Of course, projection screens are not the only source of visual resources in the worship gathering. Dramatic vignettes, use of objects to illustrate a sermon, and banners are all being used to communicate visually. Although it is word-based, preaching through story-telling has a visual element to it which appeals to the imagination as the story unfolds.

This cultural shift from hearing to seeing is having a huge impact on corporate worship. Worship leaders would do well to take a look at their worship planning from this perspective. How much visual orientation is included in the worship gathering? How might this aspect be used more effectively? For those who are regularly using presentation software for the service, evaluative questions should regularly be asked since it is a relatively new communication medium: How might its usage be improved? Is it done well with excellence? Does it adhere to solid principles of aesthetics? Are those moving backgrounds behind the song lyrics helpful or distracting to the worshipers? Adopting technology must always be followed with thoughtful evaluation as to its effectiveness in worship.

Emphasis on Community

The word "community" is a buzz-word in American life today. It even became part of the campaign platform for Barack Obama in the most recent presidential election. Even though tools for communication are advancing at a remarkable rate via internet, cell phones, satellite, and other new technologies, perhaps the proliferation of high-tech has left us feeling the need for more human touch, the need for personal connection and interaction with other human beings. Many who are searching for genuine worship experiences are also searching for churches which embody the concept of community within and beyond their corporate worship environments.

Interestingly, however, the proliferation over the last thirty years or so of worship song lyrics using singular pronouns has contributed to a heightened sense of individualism in worship. In a culture which values the "rugged individualist," American churches seem to have a diminishing understanding of the covenantal community as an important part of the church's identity. We sing our faith in terms of "I" instead of "we". Gratefully, the pendulum may be beginning to swing back toward plural pronouns in some of our new worship songs. And the swing back toward using some of the older hymns which expressed our faith in corporate form is helping to address this as well.[19]

Cultural Relevance and Worship

One of the primary reasons many church leaders decide to change certain aspects of their worship style is to become more culturally relevant. The theme of worship and cultural relevance has been discussed in a wide variety of settings in recent years.[20]

The interest in this topic often relates to helping the church reach the non-churched community. The leadership task becomes one of facilitating worship which is meaningful to those who are a part of the church (the *fold*) while at the same time appearing attractive to those who are not yet a part of the church family (the *field*), should they come. The ministry-merge of worship and evangelism has value from a biblical perspective. But the current landscape of ideas about how to accomplish it is cluttered with differing methodologies, some of which cloud an accurate understanding of authentic worship and its place in the task of evangelism.

Evaluating Church Values

For the *fold*, a major factor regarding worship is whether or not they engage with God as they come together to worship. Engaging with God, as used here, is characterized by the desire on the part of a congregation to authentically experience God in worship, to be active participants in that pursuit, and to be intentional about their worship experience. Although it is recognized that worshipers engage with God on an individual as well as a corporate level, a church in which a majority of the attendees are desiring to experience God in corporate worship and are active and intentional toward that end would be described as a congregation which is engaging with God.

A second factor for the *fold* is their openness to outsiders, those not a part of their fellowship. How hospitable are they toward those who might venture in to the worship service? How welcoming of outsiders are they as a church? This is the factor that individuals from the *field* will most readily experience as they attend a worship gathering as a guest. The sensitivity on the part of the church toward those who might visit would include such hospitality factors as friendliness, generosity, provision, and orientation.[21] Friendliness would include measures such as the way in which people were greeted and how many times they were told by someone that they were glad they had come. Generosity would be characterized by offering to help the newcomers by anticipating their needs, such as directions, childcare, or other needs. Provision would be noted by special guest parking, a welcome center, or other means of providing for the needs of those who are visiting. Orientation might include a welcome center to aid those who need information along with sensitivity on the part of service leaders to the fact that the unchurched may not understand much about how a worship service is conducted and what is expected of them. Sensitivity to language usage and other aspects of the worship "learning curve" demonstrate a church's hospitality in the orientation of their guests to an unfamiliar environment.

The following chart describes four main values, or orientations, a church may assume regarding the fold/field aspects of worship and evangelism.

CHURCH A	CHURCH B
FOLD ENGAGES WITH GOD	**FOLD** ENGAGES WITH GOD
FIELD EXPERIENCES HOSPITALITY	**FIELD** DOES NOT EXPERIENCE HOSPITALITY
CHURCH C	CHURCH D
FOLD DOES NOT ENGAGE WITH GOD	**FOLD** DOES NOT ENGAGE WITH GOD
FIELD EXPERIENCES HOSPITALITY	**FIELD** DOES NOT EXPERIENCE HOSPITALITY

Church A would be described as a church which has the right idea about biblical worship. They are interested in engaging with God in worship. They are biblical in their approach and they are involved. They value genuine worship. They also value the evangelism which results in their community being won to Christ. They don't just say it, they show it. They display a caring, sensitive hospitality to those who visit them. While never straying from the true content of worship, they are careful to facilitate it in such a way that the learning curve is not so steep, nor does it put guests on the spot or cause them to feel uncomfortable with the surroundings or how they are asked to participate.

Church B also values worship. They want to engage with God. They do not intentionally value evangelism or outreach done through the worship experience. They do not go out of their way to be hospitable to outsiders in the way they participate in worship. If someone from the outside were to visit their service, they would perhaps see people who were interested in worshiping God but they would seem focused on their own needs. They would not receive much hospitality from them, nor would they understand much about how to participate in the service. The language might sound "churchy" and they would not be instructed in how to find the Scriptures that were being referenced. They would not know how to join in on the songs that were being sung because they couldn't find the words anywhere. In short, they would almost feel like an intruder among what appeared to be a sincere group of people.

Church C values having a worship event. But they don't truly understand what that is. To them, it is a gathering, a celebration of being together. But they understand very little about biblical aspects of genuine worship. They would never say they do not engage with God, but the event is more about people than it is about honoring God. There is very little content. The preaching may emphasize felt needs of churchgoers and the community, but emphasis on God's Word may be very weak. On the other hand, they value evangelism. They value the methods of getting people to the church. They plan how they conduct the service to be very comfortable for all who attend. The guest who attends may feel very comfortable in this setting. They would be greeted warmly and attention would be paid to them. The message would be something that they could relate to: money management, family relationships, etc. But they would not have gained a very good idea of what true worship is all about from having been there. Even though they were comfortable, they never really had to interact with the content of worship. They probably would not have been presented with a picture of God as transcendent. Perhaps the up-close and personal side of God would have been emphasized.

Church D values worship only to the point that it is something they have always done. They have a routine of coming together for "worship" but they understand very little about what it means. Their service is characterized by obligatory attendance and mindless routines. They also do not seem concerned about reaching the lost community. They do not plan for outsiders to come, and they do not prepare for that possibility. If someone new comes, it is almost by accident.

All four of these characterizations exist today. Of course the healthiest is Church A, which cares about honest worship and has a heart for the lost. They don't compromise the content or water down the gospel, but they do care for those around them. They want to make the environment of worship as inviting as possible without sacrificing their identity as fully devoted followers of Christ.

When it comes to planning and leading healthy worship, the process starts with a bit of evaluation. Ask some hard questions, such as: Where is our church in this diagram? How can we be culturally relevant without sacrificing who we are as a worshiping people of God? How can we increase our corporate expression which seeks to love God with all our heart, mind, soul, and strength? And how can we love people as well?

Leading Out in Transition

When we have discovered as leaders that some changes need to take place in our corporate worship, how should we approach the task? What are the ground rules for effecting change? The following key thoughts are offered for your consideration.

First, realizing that change must be purposeful, we should avoid the trap of change for the sake of change. How obvious, you might think. But there are cases of leaders who have effected change simply because they were tired of doing things the same old way. Change to them provided a way to shake things up and pump some life into their people. Wise leaders, on the other hand, realize that change in and of itself will not solve problems. You have to identify specific areas that need to be addressed (spiritual lethargy for example) and tackle that. Just trying novel things in order to muster excitement will not address the underlying problem. It may succeed in masking the real problem for a bit longer. But it will never correct the problem. If our mission as worship leaders is to help facilitate an encounter with a holy God, then any changes we make should be aimed at accomplishing that mission.

Second, look at tradition as a tool. Recognize the validity that specific traditions once held (and perhaps still hold) in the life of the church. Traditions do need to be infused with new life sometimes, but be careful not to discard them in a wholesale fashion, believing that "tradition" is synonymous with "dead." That isn't true most of the time. The real enemy is *disengagement*. Sometimes when traditions seem lifeless, it is because the worshipers have forgotten the point. They mindlessly go through the motions without engaging with the point. That is true with most areas of our lives. The solution is to bring the point back to the attention of the people and present it in ways that resonate with them.

Remember, also, that worship is not necessarily about comfort or discomfort. The point is worshiping the true and only living God. At times, worship may be comforting and comfortable, at other times discomforting and uncomfortable as we are confronted with changes the Holy Spirit wants to make in our lives to conform us to the image of Christ. We should not be fixed on the idea of making people comfortable or uncomfortable in worship. Our task is to help them experience God, to connect with Him, to meet with Him in worship as a body of believers. That goal should be the focus of our worship planning and praying.

Sometimes we think everyone hates change. At some point in the semester we usually ask our students to respond to these questions: How many of you really dislike changes? How many of you really get pumped up about anything new that means change to you? How many of you could go either way, depending on whether or not you perceived the change to be a good one or not? Generally, a few students will indicate they don't like change. Just about as many will say they really like change, and about one-half or more will give the "either way" answer. Those percentages often work out to be about the same for people in local churches. While most people don't gravitate toward change, a large number will be willing to undergo some form of change *if they understand the purpose behind it*. The leadership lesson for us is that we need to be purposeful about change and we need to communicate those purposes in ways that make sense to people. One leader friend of mine confided that his ministry team was able to convince a segment of senior members about the need to incorporate some new styles of music in the worship service in order to reach out to the generation that included their grandchildren. That approach made sense to them, he said. As a result, they were able to move forward in healthy ways to be inclusive to all the generations of their community.

Consider another important point. People may learn to adapt to changes made, but if too many things once familiar change all at once, a sort of disequilibrium can set in. The lesson is to effect change (especially numerous and far-reaching changes) over time. Prepare your people so that they can assimilate the changes. It won't necessarily be easy, or without any hint of conflict. But it will be manageable.

Along with being a change agent, you will need to build trust. The people must know beyond any doubt that you care for them and that you have their best interest at heart. They need to hear you say that, but they also need to see you demonstrate it. This takes time. Trust-building doesn't happen overnight. So, build trust before you effect change. The church will be far more likely to support the change under those circumstances because they are in reality supporting you. They may not agree with you, but if they trust you, they will follow you more often than not.

Bring leaders in on the ideas of change. If you build consensus you will be a long way down the road in accomplishing the goals that are important. And the fun part is that you won't be doing it alone – you will enjoy doing this as a team of leaders committed to a common goal of more effectively helping your people experience God in worship. Working with a leadership team will also allow you to include more perspectives. It would be good to get a cross-section of people in this group, who will help you sift through various issues from different points of view. Some will contribute thoughts that you had not thought of before. Some will raise questions you had never considered. But this is a healthy part of the process. And it is good stewardship of the resources of the Body of Christ.

Finally, and it is mentioned last for emphasis, seek God throughout the process. Pray for His guidance in the beginning and keep on praying right through to the end. God will surely let you know His mind and heart. James reminds us that God gives us His wisdom generously and lovingly when we ask Him to help us (James 1:5).

Change is not a bad thing. In fact, Christ is in the life-changing business. We who have spent time following Him know that He doesn't leave us as we are. He wants us to become conformed into His image. He wants us to look like Him!

- What cultural shifts have you noticed in your church?
- How have you been conditioned to handle changes in your walk with God?

CHAPTER 6

Pastoring The Worshipers:
How Do We Shepherd Them?

The Personal Paradigm Shift

It was an emotional time to say the least. Events of recent days were hard to take in for everyone. Processing everything that had happened was difficult. And so the young man decided to find comfort in an activity which was both enjoyable and familiar to him. "I'm going fishing," he announced to his friends. "Why not?" they thought. They decided to join him. So away they went. But after fishing all night, they didn't catch a thing.

The next morning, still out on the water, they saw a man whom they didn't recognize standing on the lakefront. "Had any luck?" he called out to them in a friendly voice. "Not even a nibble," yelled back the young man who had spearheaded this fishless expedition. From the shore the reply came back, "Try putting the nets on the right side of the boat, and I expect you'll find some big ones!"

This unexpected fishing advice from the friendly man on shore surprised the small band of seasoned fishermen. It wasn't the advice so much that surprised them, though it was rather odd. But it reminded them of another fishing trip some three years earlier, when they had caught nothing. Like this time, they were told by a kind stranger to put their nets out again, and to their amazement, they caught so many fish that their nets began to break.

That was Peter's first encounter with Jesus. Now, as they lowered their equipment on the boat's right side, the nets began to swell with hundreds of fish! A miracle…again! Peter's friend cried out, "It's the Lord!"

Peter could hardly contain himself. Ever since he had known Jesus he had found himself jumping out of boats. (Once he had even halfway succeeded in walking on water.) But this time the rush of adrenaline fueled his speedy action. Without a second thought, he wrapped his clothes around him and jumped into the water and headed to the shore. It was Jesus!

What followed that morning was a wonderful reunion of Jesus and His disciples as they shared a breakfast of fish on the shores of Galilee. It was there that Peter received another lesson from his Lord – and a new vocation as well.

Peter thought back to that first miraculous catch of fish years earlier. Jesus had certainly gotten his attention. When he had seen all the fish breaking those nets, Peter's reaction had been one of fear; he intuitively knew he was in the presence of holiness. It scared him! In his astonishment, all Peter could do was to beg Jesus to go away. His sense of sinfulness seared his heart in the presence of Jesus. But instead of sending him away, Jesus invited Peter to become a part of His ministry. He encouraged Peter to see himself as a fisher of men (Luke 5:1-11).

And now here he was with Jesus again, but instead of talking about fish, Jesus seemed focused on sheep and lambs. "Simon, son of John, do you truly love me more than these?" "Yes," Peter replied, "you know that I love you." Then Jesus said, "Feed my lambs" (John 21:15-17).

As the question was repeated by Jesus twice more, the familiar life of boats and fishing trips began to recede in his mind. The focus was shifting from catching fish to feeding lambs. His old identity as a fisherman was being replaced with a new identity as someone who cared for sheep: a pastor!

Jesus often used the analogy of sheep and shepherd in talking about spiritual leadership. He referred to Himself as the Good Shepherd (John 10:11). He furthered the analogy to include His disciples as shepherds (or pastors) in working with the church body.

As worship leaders, we are called to the great work of shepherding the flock. Both when we plan and lead worship services, we are leading sheep. What do we need to remember as we work with the sheep in our congregation? First, we need to remember that, in worship, *the sheep need a shepherd.*

Sheep Like to Wander

It is no wonder that the Bible makes several references to people as sheep. Isaiah reminded us of our human tendency to get off-track and wander away from the path. "We all, like sheep, have gone astray; each of us has turned to his own way..." (Isa. 53:6). Hymn-writers as well have alluded to this sheep-like tendency. The well-known nineteenth-century hymn says it well: "Jesus sought me when a stranger, wandering from the fold of God" and "Prone to wander, Lord, I feel it; prone to leave the God I love."[22] Our twenty-first century culture might easily be characterized by that same analysis.

To understand the process of shepherding, it is helpful to realize this characteristic of ourselves and the people whom we desire to lead. We get distracted and wander off easily. The influence of a media-saturated culture has contributed to short attention spans, and adults and children alike are being medicated for Attention Deficit Syndrome at an unprecedented rate. The ability of people to focus on one central activity has become a challenge while multi-tasking is the norm. For multi-taskers, focusing on one central activity is a challenge in itself.

In our contemporary world, even the way people process information has shifted radically from linear to non-linear thought patterns. The use of internet-based research processes has contributed to this phenomenon.

A worship pastor understands the need to plan and lead worship in ways that are able to minister to the very real challenges of contemporary society.

A Flock of Many Different Sheep

Jesus knows His sheep well (John 10:14). But who exactly are these sheep anyway? It is probably safe to say that every congregation possesses a certain level of diversity within its membership. Factors such as generational cohort, education level, socio-economic condition, and ethnicity contribute to the multi-faceted nature of a congregation. Any one of these factors, as well as others, could affect the degree of diversity within the congregation. For example, the diversity within a church comprised of people of various age groups under the same roof – Elders, Builders, Boomers, GenXers, and Mosaics (GenY) – might pose some special challenges for worship planners.[23]

A need for unity has always existed in the church. Jesus Himself prayed for His disciples to have it as well as for those of us who would come along much later in history. Does unity mean "uniformity"? No, the rich and poor were still rich and poor; the old and young were still old and young; and the man and woman were still man and woman in the church. Then what does unity mean? It is something that transcends human culture. It is not found in our attributes. It is found through Christ. Our unity is found in Him. Our identity in Him is the common denominator for those who have been redeemed, those of every tongue and tribe, every creed and age. We are made one in Christ.

As a worship leader, get to know the flock. Your ministry is effective to the degree that you help a diverse group connect with one common objective: attributing worth to God!

Sheep Are Vulnerable

Just as sheep in the open fields are vulnerable to predators, sheep in the church are at risk as well. There is an enemy, a "roaring lion," who does not want them to worship God in spirit and in truth. He will try to create confusion in their lives regarding worship.

It should not surprise any church leader that the church would face controversy over issues of worship. The sometimes subtle source of these conflicts, Satan, does not want Christians to experience the fullness of God in corporate worship. The enemy knows that the foundation for powerful living begins with a right relationship with God through experiencing Him as both Savior and Sovereign Lord. Since worship is the sincere attitude and expression of those spiritual realities in the believer's life, leaders need to be aware of three primary tactics the enemy uses to stoke the fires of worship discontent among the sheep: (1) a faulty understanding of worship (2) ineffective leadership, and (3) comparison shopping.

The first of these enemy tactics has swept through many churches with hurricane force winds. Its worship mantra has been repeated many times in various ways: Worship is "what I like" and "how I like it." The enemy has worked overtime to promote the lie that worship is about our personal preferences. Particularly focusing our attention on musical style, but on other issues as well, Satan has carefully tried to escort us away from the central truth of worship as a recognition of God as Creator and Sovereign Lord and of our spiritual need to bow before Him in adoration.

Another favorite tactic centers on the worship leaders themselves. Those called to lead in worship from the platform have a tremendous responsibility before God and to their congregations. They are not only worship leaders but lead-worshipers as well. Worship pastors are not just doing a paid "gig." They care for the people God has entrusted to their care and seek to disciple them in experiencing true, Spirit-filled worship. Caring leaders will intercede for their people in prayer.

If the enemy can in any way discredit the leader, then the congregation will be distracted from the task of worshipping. Sometimes, unfortunately, leaders discredit themselves by unholy living. Then the act of leading others becomes nothing more than a charade. Worship leaders must guard their hearts against impurity and unholy living. Those who would lead others must be living authentically. Sometimes leaders are unfairly attacked by individuals in the church. Worship leaders are not immune to the effects of gossip and slander. Being "wise as serpents and harmless as doves" is an important part of leadership. Leaders would do well to remember, however, who the real enemy is and that his primary goal is to sandbag any healthy expression of worship in the church.

A third common tactic the enemy employs in his pursuit of non-worship is encouraging church members to compare what their church is doing in worship to the churches all around them. This comparison-shopping may lead to church-hopping – "going where the action is."

The Sheep Belong to God: A Comforting Thought

God entrusts the flock to leaders as "under-shepherds" but ultimately they belong to Him. As worship leaders we would do well to remember that it is God's kingdom, God's work, God's call on our lives, and God's flock! Although He demands our very best efforts as His co-laborers, He alone is the source of strength and wisdom for the church. This is good news for leaders! The burden does not rest on our shoulders. The spiritual well-being of every member of the flock is ultimately God's responsibility, not ours. It is a relief to know that, in the end, the sheep belong to God. There is a higher authority than the worship pastor. When I fail them, God can still intervene in their lives. Does that diminish our responsibility to be faithful? Not in the least. But it does release us from suffering a ministerial martyr complex. There is only one Messiah – Jesus Christ, the Good Shepherd, who laid down His life for the sheep.

As a reminder of how much God thinks of His sheep, read Matthew 18:12-13. It's the story of a man who owned one hundred sheep, and one of them got lost. What did the man do? He left the flock in search of the missing sheep. Why did he do it? The sheep missing mattered more than the flock gathered. That story should leave little doubt as to how God feels about each person He created. The challenge for leaders is to value each individual as much as God does.

The Sheep Belong to God: A Challenging Thought

Some time ago we had the opportunity to spend a week at a camp in rural Cuba teaching for a pastor's conference. During the day a herd of goats would wander around the lush hillsides as they grazed. Observing them, a particular feature about these goats was discovered. Besides being wonderful "lawnmowers" wherever they went, they produced a nasal-like bleating sound. "Baah...Baah." (You have to use your imagination.) The antiphonal sound of these animals was amusing. That is, all but one. It seems there was one goat that had a distinct bleat. It was lower-pitched and more edgy than the rest. More like "Bawh...Bawh." And it was annoying! Although there were approximately fifty goats bleating constantly, that single sound stuck out as an irritation!

Because sheep also are known to bleat, the task of leadership is not an easy one at times. Occasions arise when those whom we seek to lead can make our job difficult or irritating at the least. Most leaders experience those times when they want to give up doing what God has called them to do. Why is this? Usually it has something to do with the bleating of the sheep we are trying to lead.

According to definition, to "bleat" is to "talk complainingly or with a whine." If we were to translate some of those bleating sounds regarding worship, the results might include these familiar translations:

Baah... "I didn't like that we had to stand up for three songs in a row ."

Baah... "The sermon went too long this morning."

Baah... "Do we have to sing so many new songs?"

Baah... "Do we have to sing so many old songs?"

Baah... "I hate the sound of the drums in worship!"

Baah... "Does the organ have to play that loudly?"

You get the picture. There are any number of "bleats" that could be translated. Unless you are working with a very spiritually mature flock, you can expect bleating as a part of the ministry challenge. A worship leader should keep in mind that it is the nature of sheep to make bleating sounds. And, out of fairness to the sheep, a moment of personal reflection will probably remind us that we, the leaders, like to bleat occasionally as well! A good under-shepherd cares for the sheep despite the irritating noises they make, remembering that each sheep is unconditionally loved by God.

Sheep Like to Be Fed

Peter's paradigm shift from fisherman to shepherd was monumental. In dealing with the fish, all he had to do was gather them up and get them to shore where someone else would get them to market. It was fairly cut and dried (no pun intended) with limited involvement with the fish. Being a shepherd, on the other hand, demanded much more personal involvement. The sheep were a full-time job and they had to be cared for. They had to be led to places where they could graze and also receive the water that was so necessary for their health and survival.

What Do We Feed Them?

So what do we feed them? What is on the menu as we plan worship services and lead them week by week in corporate worship? The real heart of worship leadership is discerning what the flock needs as they gather together to honor the Lord. Their primary need, of course, is to engage with God. If they don't do that, then all else is futile. But it doesn't just happen automatically. As pastoral leaders of worship, we help our people even before they gather corporately by discipling them in an understanding of what genuine worship is. We help them integrate the truth into their lives that worship is more than just an hour on Sunday; it is a life-style of giving praise and thanks to God. We help them understand what Paul wrote to the Colossian church: "And whatever you do, whether in word or deed, do it all in the name of the Lord Jesus, giving thanks to God the Father through him" (Col. 3:17).

In our planning, we make sure the main ingredients are there: a celebration of the greatness and glory of God and a grateful awareness of the salvation he has provided for us through Jesus Christ, our Hope of eternal glory. We help them feast on a balanced content of seeing God as the High King of heaven as well as our merciful, loving Savior. God is both transcendent and immanent; above and beyond us, yet with us (Emmanuel). Our worship planning and leading should reflect both of those incredible truths.

So How Do We Feed Them?

As we plan, we need to make sure that we are using the basic building blocks of a worship gathering (the elements) in ways that engage people with God. Including these elements will ensure that worshipers have ample opportunity to connect with God during the worship gathering in various ways. Hopefully, they will experience God through the reading of Scripture and preaching. Hopefully they will delight in Him as they praise Him via music and other forms of testimony. They may commit themselves anew to Him while giving their tithes and offerings. They may respond to Him in open invitation as they are challenged by His Word. And they may remember again what He has done for them personally through the observance of the Lord's Table and through seeing new believers being baptized. Through the Holy Spirit, each of these elements can help worshipers engage with God in ways that will bring Him glory and transform their lives.

The design of the service is a tool as well to help people meet with God in the corporate setting. The carefully developed and prayed-over plan helps the worshipers as they move through the various phases of worship. The progression of gathering together, praising God, confessing our need, focusing on what God is saying to us, hearing His Word preached, responding to what has been heard, and transitioning to live out the faith in the context of daily lives can be enhanced by a worship service which is well-designed. It is a tool which can be used to help people both think and feel deeply about God and about others around them. When a worship gathering is filled with worshipers whose worship is authentic, it is anything but a routine.

Fostering a Community

Helping worshipers experience the dual dimensions of worship is an important facet of the work of worship leaders. Our planning and leading should aim toward ushering people into the throne room of heaven while helping them to relate to others as a part of the community of the redeemed. Sometimes we focus so much on the vertical element of worship that we neglect the horizontal (community relationship) dimension. Corporate worship is both/and— which includes the community aspect. Worshipers are built up and encouraged by one another in the context of praising God together. Just being together and encouraging and praying for one another are important components of corporate worship. An emphasis on "we" instead of "me" points to community. Although there is a place for both singular and plural pronouns in our worship songs, at least some of the song lyrics should express the community aspect – the "we" of the worshiping community. The gathered flock is diverse in many ways, but we are brought together and unified under one central theme: Christ has redeemed us from our sins! This is the single greatest common denominator of all!

When the Shepherd Feels Empty

With all the myriad of details and concepts surrounding the topic of worship and worship leadership, it is very possible that we might feel overwhelmed at the task of preparing and leading a congregation in this pursuit. We might be tempted to throw up our hands in frustration, feeling as if we are in way over our heads. From a human perspective, that is certainly true. We are in over our heads. Attempting to engage the congregation in corporate worship requires many more resources than we have on our own.

Late one day, as night was approaching, a hungry crowd was gathered in a remote place. Thousands of men, women, and children had no food to eat and no place to buy any. A few men noticed the situation and went to suggest to their leader how the needs might be met. Their solution was to send the crowd away so they could buy some food for themselves. It sounded to them like a great plan. What else could they do? They had no food to give the people.

How startled they must have been at Jesus' response. He told them: "You give them something to eat!"

"We have only five loaves and two fish," they answered in shock (Luke 9:13).

Their minds reeled at the ridiculous thought of dividing a sack lunch of two sardines and five small bread rolls among a crowd of thousands. There was no way! Why would He suggest such a thing?

Then, right there before their human eyes, they witnessed a divine miracle. They saw Jesus do something that they never could have imagined! They saw Him take the meager resources they had, thank God for them, break them, and then give them back to them for distribution to the crowd. It went on in a seemingly endless multiplication! Fish and bread, fish and bread, more fish and bread, until everyone was fed! And if that were not enough, when they had finished, there were twelve baskets of leftovers, a souvenir for each of the leaders to remind them that human resources are never enough to get the job done. But we have more than just human resources. We have the resources of Jesus Christ available to us through the Holy Spirit to help us as we anticipate, plan and pray for our HOLY GATHERINGS.

- What does Jesus' use of the story of the ten sheep say to you as a worship leader?
- Who stands out in your mind as an excellent example of a worthy leader who shepherds the congregation?

CHAPTER 7

Evaluating Worship:
How Can We Improve It?

Just the mere mention of worship evaluation troubles some of us. How can we evaluate what's going on between God and His people in a worship service? Only He is qualified to do something so audacious, we say to ourselves, so evaluating worship can't ever be seen as our business.

Yet, a congregation's worship has to be evaluated in order to be improved, and whether we're comfortable with it or not, worship leaders have to do it. Granted, we can't evaluate what goes on between the Lord and His people as they gather together to meet Him. But at the same time, we can – and must – evaluate how we lead people into His presence and how well they follow our leadership. Like all worthwhile evaluation processes, the product is a list of areas of improvement. If we take them seriously, we will lead better, and in turn, God's people will follow better. As a result, worship that transforms God's people will be that much more possible.

Pastoral Evaluation

When we think about worship evaluation, we usually bring up technical issues like the use of sound or projection systems, the quality of the music, or the skill of the preacher. Indeed, these issues deserve serious consideration and will be brought up later in this chapter. However, worship evaluation also involves other important issues that aren't necessarily characterized as technical. These issues are typically associated with spiritual and relational realities, and evaluating them means incorporating ministry gifts and skills generally associated with pastoral ministry. However, any worship leader who works lovingly and faithfully with a congregation should be able to assess the issues isolated in this critical part of the evaluation process.

Speaking of the pastor and worship, many ministers consider the work of evaluation to be the responsibility of the person whose ministry assignment has to do with the actual task of planning and leading the service. Consequently, worship leaders skilled in music selection and preparation or service design and production can be left to shoulder the load of evaluation by themselves. Pastors may not be involved in evaluation because they don't have a grasp of the technical details of worship design and leadership. In other words, they probably don't know very much about modulating music, rehearsing with musicians, transitioning within the service, or tweaking the sound system for the benefit of the worship experience.

Knowing little or nothing about the technical aspects of worship leadership, however, doesn't excuse a pastor from being involved in evaluation. In fact, some of the most critical issues in worship evaluation are addressed best by pastors or ministers who have pastoral gifts and skills.

In reality, the pastor is the main worship leader. It's an assignment assumed in the pastor's role as an equipping leader in the church (Eph. 4:11-13). Such an assertion doesn't imply that the pastor is responsible for choosing the songs, working the sound system, or handling the other technical details for the service. Rather, it means that the pastor is responsible for making sure that the people in his congregation worship the Lord in a way that's based on rock-solid theology. The pastor also has to take the responsibility for assuring that Christ-centered relationships will be strengthened in the church through what happens in worship. For these reasons, a pastor does well to participate in the process of evaluating worship services.

What's involved in worship evaluation for a pastor? The following areas suggest the doctrinal and relational dimensions of worship that deserve a pastor's attention. Of course, the areas considered do not represent an exhaustive list. Hopefully, other areas will come to mind for a pastor who works through the process of evaluating the following areas of worship.

Leaders

Two questions serve well to evaluate the leaders of worship. Neither of these questions could be considered technical in nature. Rather, they go to the heart of the leader, a component that can be overlooked if worship leaders evaluate the technical issues of the service alone.

1. To what extent do the worship leaders know how to come into the presence of God themselves so they can lead God's people to come into His presence as well?
2. How much do the worship leaders show that they love the people in their congregation enough to keep on trying to lead them to encounter God in worship?

These two questions intertwine to form a focus of evaluation that can render important information for the worship leaders. The information can help them to improve in ways that can't always be measured in technical ways.

The first question stimulates a worship leader to evaluate his or her relationship with God. Figuratively speaking, we can't take people to a meeting with God if we don't know how to get there ourselves. Consequently, we do our best work as worship leaders when we ourselves devote serious attention to personal encounters with God on a regular basis.

Carol had been suffering for a long time with a paralyzing disease, and the struggle was taking its toll on her spiritually as well as physically and emotionally. She longed to be well enough to hold her new baby, to hug her husband, and to clasp her hands in prayer. But so far, her body didn't seem to be getting better. In fact, she knew that she was getting worse.

Lying on her hospital bed one night, she wept in despair over her condition. Her nurse came into her room, saw her tears, and leaned in close to her and whispered softly in her ear, "Carol, would you mind if I prayed for you?"

"Please pray for me," Carol replied with anguish seeping through her voice. "Please, please pray for me."

Quietly but confidently, her nurse got on her knees next to Carol, placed her hand on Carol's troubled forehead, and then began to pray. Later Carol remarked about what happened to her as her nurse prayed for her. "At that moment that nurse took me to a place where she had been many times before," Carol testified, "and she knew how to take me there with her."

In a way, guiding God's people in worship can be characterized by the same experience, but only if the worship leaders themselves follow the example of Carol's nurse. Knowing the path to worship personally is an absolute necessity if we intend to guide God's people into His presence corporately. Of course, God's Spirit actually does the guiding, and the worship leaders who take their cues from Him will be effective in leading others in worship. But again, following His leadership in private worship can make a huge difference in a worship leader's sensitivity to Him in planning and leading congregational worship.

The second question also gets at the critical issue of the heart. If worship leaders love the people in the congregation, a distinct evidence of it will be their determination to keep on trying to find ways to help the people so they can worship the Lord. A loving heart produces the indomitable determination that won't allow a minister to give up on God's people. By contrast, a lack of love for the church will show up in the way a minister gives up on the people and on the hope that they will have life-transforming meetings with God when they gather together for worship.

Accordingly, worship leaders should examine whether we love the people God has given to us. If our love for them is growing, so will our resolve to work hard to help them have meaningful encounters with God. However, if we don't love them, then that sad fact should be an important matter of prayer. Asking God to show us how to allow His love to fill our hearts will go a long way toward changing us so we can do justice to the ministry with the people to whom He has called us.

Purpose

A couple of questions regarding the purpose of worship can be raised in our evaluation. These questions address the doctrinal foundation of worship and the appropriate practical application of it in the church.

1. To what extent have the people in the congregation embraced the purpose of worship as a life-transforming encounter with God?
2. How is their awareness of the purpose of worship being reflected in the services?

Like the previous pair of questions, these points of inquiry intermingle to direct worship leaders to some vital considerations that need to be evaluated.

The first question assumes that the worship leaders have embraced the purpose of worship as being a meeting with God. It also is built on the reality that worship leaders have devoted themselves to guiding their people in the service so that such a life-transforming encounter may be possible.

Given that assumption, answering the first question exposes some fundamental observations about the congregation. In particular, it causes the worship leaders to observe the actual purposes of the regular Sunday gatherings of God's people. As the question implies, congregations gather at the church for a number of reasons, and some of them don't have very much to do with meeting God. Instead, they have more to do with meeting each other, engaging in a long-standing community tradition, or promoting a particular agenda. With their behavior, worship leaders can also portray an alternate purpose for gathering. We can behave in ways that give the distinct impression that the worship service is about meeting us.

Although the question is provocative, it's not intended to be caustic. Answering it doesn't have to give way to a reprimand of the congregation from the pulpit. Rather, it can guide the worship leaders to observe some issues to be addressed as they teach God's people about the Christ-centered purpose of gathering together as a worshiping congregation. In turn, addressing these issues through instruction in God's ways can help God's people go a long way toward maturity in worship.

The next question forces worship leaders to evaluate a church's perception of the purpose of gathering together in realistic terms. All too often, worship leaders are not all that different from the people in the pews when it comes to worship evaluation. We judge a service or any feature in it based on what we like or what we dislike. And usually the judgment that's made is based on emotional responses or culture-bound preferences.

Listing the objective ways which demonstrate that congregations have embraced the purpose of worship can be a little risky. The list will be only as reliable as the worship leaders who develop it. Hopefully, we will think through the question carefully in light of doctrinal clarity and relational maturity. The list should show that the items on it resonate with the truths of Scripture about God's people and reflect the importance of healthy relationships in the church with Him and His people. Accordingly, the list would include items such as:

- An eagerness to allow people to respond publicly during the invitation
- A willingness to set aside time constraints
- A tendency to talk with one another before and after worship
- A desire to obey and serve the Lord
- A concern for people who aren't Christians

- An enthusiasm about praying for others
- An anticipation of spiritual transformation

Of course, this list is not exhaustive. However, it suggests the kinds of tangible expressions of worship in which God's people have embraced the purpose for gathering together.

Structure

An entire chapter in this book has been devoted to designing worship services. In that chapter, attention was given to developing congregational worship opportunities that reflect movement through distinct phases that have sound theological footing. These phases of movement have been described in various ways by a number of worship theorists, but they have been identified in this book as gathering, praising, confessing, focusing, preaching, inviting, and departing.

A service designed in keeping with these phases provides a sense of movement through the worship experience. The result is a sense of direction that nurtures an environment more favorable for an encounter with the Lord. By the same token, services designed without regard for consideration for appropriate phases of movement through worship will likely render an experience that's haunted by an unrelenting lack of direction. For that reason, worship leaders should evaluate the way the services are designed to make sure that they are planned properly. Consequently, two questions need to be addressed with regard to worship structure:

1. To what extent does the structure of the services reflect phases of movement that are theologically reliable?
2. How can the structure of the services be improved to accommodate movement through the worship experience?

These questions suggest a basic two-step evaluation process involving isolation of areas of improvement and incorporating them into the worship services.

The first question implies that worship leaders will evaluate service designs according to the template provided in the models that are either prescribed or described in the Bible. Passages like Isaiah 6:1-8 and Psalm 95:1-8 reflect some obvious phases of movement which serve well to give worship leaders some helpful clues about how God's people can be led to move through a service. Tracking the phases of the encounters with God portrayed in these passages and others like them can be a great starting point for developing a design template that will guide worship leaders through the planning process.

Without the second question, however, the evaluation of worship at the point of structure will not be as productive. Worship leaders who take the necessary step of asking about how the structure can improve will make better use of this important portion of the evaluation process.

Worship leaders have found that considering the question about improvement seems to point to one critical area: transitioning within the service. It's the area that involves the way worship leaders guide God's people into, through, and out of a service effectively. Some worship leaders give serious attention to it, while others ignore it. Those who take transitions seriously help themselves to a valuable tool for effective worship leadership.

Guiding God's people in worship can be compared to leading a tour of a museum. An effective tour guide knows how to guide the visitors from one station to another within the museum. Effective leadership means guiding the tour so that everyone enjoys an enriching experience and no one gets lost along the way. Guiding visitors to approach, stop, and then exit each station in sequence smoothly requires a tour guide to learn the fine art of transitioning them carefully using little more than words and gestures. It also means that the tour guide understands how each station along the way connects in shaping the overall experience of the visitors who come to the museum.

In more than a few ways, worship leadership has nothing in common with guiding a tour through a museum. However, the analogy clarifies the value of transitioning God's people well through the experiences of worship. And it also demonstrates that worship leaders have some distinct tools to use in the process. These tools include words and gestures shaped in the form of verbal instructions, songs, Scripture readings, and prayers.

An example of growing stronger in transitions involves preachers. In worship designed to take preaching seriously, God's people are led into this critical phase of the service with great care. Usually, the worship leaders will plan a particularly distinct contribution to the service just prior to the sermon in order to help the congregation to focus on the Scripture and the proclamation of it in worship. In many services, these contributions take the form of well-rehearsed songs contributed by a choir, a praise team, a performance group, or a vocal and/or an instrumental soloist. Although the form may be different, the effort performed well reflects a desire for God to use the contribution to prepare God's people to hear the sermon.

If you're the preacher, you owe it to the congregation to see the importance of what's happened in worship so far and its connection with what you are about to do as you stand and preach your sermon. When you go to the pulpit, you will have been given the attention of a congregation that has been led to focus on what you intend to say as you preach. In a way, you have been given the baton in a relay race, and your turn has come to take it and run with it. In another way, you have been given the people who have been led through the worship experience to your station. Now you must lead them from there.

If you are not wise, you will drop the baton by ignoring what the other worship leaders have done in order to get it into your hands. Or, to see it another way, you will run the risk of losing the people who have been transitioned to you not long after they arrive at your station in the worship service. If you start your sermon with an obligatory joke that has nothing to do with the service or the sermon, you can rest assured that the baton will fall out of your grasp. Likewise, if you begin your sermon with a prefabricated introduction that's not connected with what has happened in the worship experience, you will likely squander the opportunity given to you to capitalize on the attention of God's people who have been led to your station.

The example of preaching serves well to show the value of evaluating transitions in order to improve them. In addition, evaluating the structure will reveal other areas of improvement. Setting goals to improve worship based on the evaluation and working toward them will make the service better. In turn, the congregation at worship will grow stronger.

Congregation

Speaking of the congregation, worship leaders must also evaluate God's people as well. After all, worship isn't only about what the leaders do to prompt people to meet God. It involves what the congregation does in terms of knowing the Lord and living according to His ways. Most important, it's about the relationship that each person in the pew has with the Lord Jesus Christ. Consequently, worship evaluation has to include the assessment of the spiritual maturity of the people who gather together on Sunday.

Two questions to evaluate the spiritual maturity of the congregation come to mind:

1. How healthy is the congregation?
2. What discipleship needs should be met in order for the congregation to engage in meaningful worship?

The spiritual health of the congregation will play a significant role in worship that makes a difference in the lives of the people. Equally true, identifying the discipleship needs within the congregation can make a difference in the way the people worship the Lord together.

The first question relates to one of the most helpful issues in church leadership today. For years, church growth occupied the attention of ministers everywhere. Recently, however, our attention has been turned to the health of the church. We have become concerned about how the congregation strives to be a healthy reflection of the body of Christ.

As we have to come to understand, church health is expressed in the way a congregation fulfills some basic and interrelated functions. Most of the literature on church health identifies the functions as worship, evangelism, discipleship, ministry, and fellowship.[24] Healthy congregations don't deal with these functions as separate concerns. Rather these issues are connected to one another in the same way that the circulatory, skeletal, respiratory, and other systems function together to keep the human body healthy. Accordingly, worship has to be evaluated with the other functions of a healthy congregation in mind.

One way to place the evaluation of a congregation's worship in the context of church health is to raise the following questions in sequence:

1. How healthy is the congregation in terms of evangelism, discipleship, fellowship, and ministry as well as worship?
2. What health needs in the congregation exist that should be dealt with so worship will be better?

Taken in order, both questions guide worship leaders to examine the congregation and then to isolate some health issues to be addressed. Dealing with them will result in worship that portrays a healthy congregation gathering for an encounter with God which is filled with potential for spiritual transformation.

A key assumption accompanies the first question. The worship leaders assume that worship isn't the exclusive focus of congregational life. For some worship leaders, that assumption cannot be accepted. For them, the church exists solely to worship God. Such a perspective excludes everything except worship from the list of important functions of the congregation. They go on to argue that all of the other functions emanate from worship. Their perspective, therefore, doesn't lead them to see church health as an integration of various functions that are equally important to the health of a congregation.

However, worship leaders who see the value of the church health perspective place what happens in worship in the context of what's going on with the congregation as a whole. Such a holistic analysis can show the obvious and vital connections between worship and the other functions. Consequently, it can reveal weaknesses in other functions of the church that are having a negative effect on what's happening – or not happening – in worship.

The second question helps worship leaders to isolate areas of need which are perhaps not directly involved in the gatherings themselves. Addressing them, however, will have a direct effect on the way the congregation worships. For instance, worship leaders may notice that the congregation needs to be more intentional about evangelism. Addressing that concern may mean directing the attention and involvement of the congregation in efforts aimed directly at sharing the good news of Christ with people in the community, at far-away mission settings, or both. As a result of the effort, the people involved in evangelizing their world bring their new burden for people and their desire to serve God by sharing Christ with others with them to worship. Their hearts stirred by the spiritual ambition to see people saved will have a direct influence on how they worship the Lord who saves.

Other needs may emerge in the evaluation of worship as a component of church health. Needs like those on the following list may focus the attention of worship leaders in order to strengthen what happens when the congregation gathers on Sunday:

- The need to forgive someone in the congregation
- The need to surrender to Him
- The need to wait on the Lord
- The need to pray for others
- The need to be concerned about people who have not received Christ
- The need to live in expectancy that God is at work in the lives of His people
- The need to look forward to the return of Christ
- The need to trust God in every situation
- The need to step out in faith as an act of obedience to Christ

- The need to repent of unconfessed sin

Will addressing these needs have an impact on what happens in worship? Absolutely! As God's people grow toward maturity in Him, the more likely that their worship experiences will foster a life-transforming encounter with God.

As you can see, a pastoral evaluation of worship related to the leadership, the purpose, the structure, and the congregation is necessary. By engaging in it, worship leaders can take a long, hard look at the spiritual issues so important to a healthy church. For the pastor beginning the process of such an evaluation, a couple of considerations will require some thought:

- How would you conduct a pastoral evaluation of the worship in your church?
- Who would you enlist to help you with such an evaluation process?

POSTLUDE

WHAT'S NEXT?

We couldn't finish the book without a few closing comments. Like we said at the beginning of the book, what you have read is the product of our work so far in the area of worship. We have tried to do justice to some of the basic issues related to leading God's people into an encounter with Him.

As you reflect on what we have offered on the subject, we are sure that you will notice that we didn't cover everything. We noticed it too. One area in particular kept nudging us to take another step forward. It's the area of worship that's been largely overlooked in our attempt to examine worship as a congregational event.

The area to which we now turn our attention is worship as a lifestyle. Regrettably, when we talk about worship as an event, we bring to the table the issues you have encountered in the chapters of this book. But worship as an event for a congregation will only be meaningful across time when God's people embrace the necessity of worshiping God as a lifestyle priority.

So keep in mind that more will be said about worship as a lifestyle. For now, remember that the concerns we raised and addressed in congregational worship have been based on the assumption that God's people are devoted to Him and eager to come into His presence. In the future, we intend to address that assumption.

Thank the Lord for allowing you to come into His presence as one of His children. Along with others who adore Him, look forward to the HOLY GATHERINGS of His people in worship.

NOTES

1 Graham Kendrick, "Meekness and Majesty," Make Way Music, Ltd/ Thankyou Music Admin. by Maranatha! Music, 1986.

2 Eliza E. Hewitt, "Sunshine in My Soul," Public Domain hymn text.

3 For example, see James White, *Introduction to Christian Worship,* 3rd ed. (Nashville: Abingdon Press, 2000); Robert Webber, *Worship Old and New,* 3rd ed. (Grand Rapids: Zondervan, 1994); Franklin Segler and Randall Bradley, *Christian Worship: Its Theology and Practice* (Nashville: Broadman and Holman, 2006).

4 In the biblical sense, praise refers to the action of declaring the worth of God—His character and His mighty acts in creation, redemption, and ongoing care for His children. Though the word has become synonymous with "music" in many Christian churches, the concept of praise extends beyond musical expression. One may praise God with or without the tool of musical expression, because praise, or declaring God's worth, can be expressed in both musical *and* non-musical ways.

5 Andrew Hill, *Enter His Courts with Praise: Old Testament Worship for the New Testament Church* (Grand Rapids: Baker Books, 1993), 127.

6 Just a few of the works addressing the topic include: Elmer L. Towns, *Putting an End to Worship Wars* (Nashville: Broadman & Holman, 1996); Carol Doran and H. Troeger Thomas, *Trouble at the Table: Gathering the Tribes for Worship* (Nashville: Abingdon Press, 1992); Steve Miller, *The Contemporary Christian Music Debate: Worldly Compromise or Agent of Renewal?* (Wheaton, IL: Tyndale House,

1993); Andy Langford, *Transitions in Worship* (Nashville: Abingdon Press, 1999); Terry W. York, *America's Worship Wars* (Peabody, MA: Hendrickson Publishers, 2003); Barry Liesch, *The New Worship: Straight Talk on Music and the Church,* expanded ed. (Grand Rapids: Baker Book House, 2001).

7   For more information on historical styles of liturgical practice, see the article by Lloyd Patterson "Worship during the Fourth and Fifth Centuries," in *The Complete Library of Christian Worship, Vol. 2: Twenty Centuries of Christian Worship* (Nashville: Star Song Publishing Group, 1994).

8   In his book *America's Worship Wars*, York has pointed out that an understanding of the tensions between culture and worship practice is central to understanding why churches have faced such upheaval regarding worship.

9   Søren Kierkegaard, *Purity of Heart is to Will One Thing* (New York: Harper, 1956), 180-81.

10   See Psalm 9:1; 52:9; 107:8 for representative passages which use the Hebrew word transliterated as *yadah.*

11   For a better understanding of the history of the church conflict over musical styles, see York's *America's Worship Wars* (Peabody, MA: Hendrickson Publishers, 2003).

12   The Genevan Psalter contains the repertory of this group of worshipers. An example which has survived to this day, and included in many American hymnals, is OLD ONE HUNDREDTH, known in some evangelical churches as the "Doxology."

13   Musical notes, rhythms, and other elements which create musical styles do not possess morality in and of themselves any more than the colors of a spectrum do; that is, they are amoral. However, nonmusical association with a *particular* musical element could potentially carry a moral or ethical association, depending upon the context. For example, Sr. Miyares from Cuba explained that hearing a Christian lyric set to a particular Cuban musical style (*ritmo*) immediately caused him to think of his life before knowing Christ and the pagan lifestyle associated with the musical idiom. As he stated, this music was not edifying to him because of its prior association in his life.

14   Bob Dylan, "The Times They Are a-Changin'," Special Rider Music, 1963.

15   For a classic discussion on the topic of the relationship between Christ and culture, see H. Richard Niebuhr, *Christ and Culture* (New York, NY: Harper and Row, 1951).

16   Leonard Sweet, "A New Reformation: Re-Creating Worship for a Postmodern World," in *Experience God in Worship*, ed. Michael Warden (Group Publishing, 2000), 173.

17   Robert Webber, *Worship is a Verb: Eight Principles for Transforming Worship* (Peabody, Mass: Hendrickson, 1992).

18   George Barna, "Technology Use is Growing Rapidly in Churches." Available online at www.barna.org/.

19   In the past couple of years several well-known contemporary Christian artists have released recording projects featuring classic hymn texts. Examples include Jars of Clay, MercyMe, Passion Worship Band, Third Day, and Avalon, among others.

20   Sally Morgenthaler's *Worship Evangelism* (Grand Rapids: Zondervan, 1996) is a seminal resource on the topic.

21   More on this topic is available in *The Art of Personal Evangelism* by Will McRaney (Nashville: Broadman and Holman, 2003).

22   Robert Robinson, "Come, Thou Fount of Every Blessing," Public Domain hymn text.

23   For an excellent overview of these generational cohorts, refer to *Boiling Point* by George Barna and Mark Hatch (Regal Books, 2001).

24   Rick Warren, *The Purpose-Driven Church* (Grand Rapids, MI: Zondervan, 1995), 103-109; Reginald McDonough, ed., *Leading Your Church in Long-Range Planning* (Nashville, TN: Convention Press, 1975).

CPSIA information can be obtained
at www.ICGtesting.com
Printed in the USA
BVHW060039100920
588458BV00005B/215

9 781432 740740